LEARNING THINGS

LEARNING THINGS

Material Culture in Art Education

Doug Blandy
Paul E. Bolin

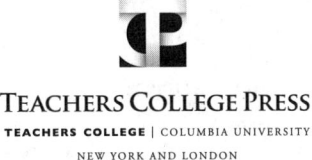

TEACHERS COLLEGE PRESS
TEACHERS COLLEGE | COLUMBIA UNIVERSITY
NEW YORK AND LONDON

Published by Teachers College Press, 1234 Amsterdam Avenue, New York, NY 10027

Copyright © 2018 by Teachers College, Columbia University

Cover photos: Type case by Skeezer via Getty Images. Kente cloth by Adam Jones; fishing lures by Ilkka Jukarainen; coins by David Holt; buttons by A Little Creation; animal figurines by Garrison Gunter; silver tribal necklace by Ann Porteus; marbles by Candace Wright Nelms, all via Flickr under a creative commons attribution license.

All rights reserved. No part of this publication may be reproduced or transmitted in any form or by any means, electronic or mechanical, including photocopy, or any information storage and retrieval system, without permission from the publisher. For reprint permission and other subsidiary rights requests, please contact Teachers College Press, Rights Dept.: tcpressrights@tc.columbia.edu

Library of Congress Cataloging-in-Publication Data

Names: Blandy, Douglas Emerson, 1951- author. | Bolin, Paul Erik, 1954- author.
Title: Learning things : material culture in art education / Doug Blandy, Paul E. Bolin.
Description: New York, NY : Teachers College Press, [2018] | Includes bibliographical references and index.
Identifiers: LCCN 2018004216|
ISBN 9780807759196 (paper : acid-free paper)
ISBN 9780807777022 (ebook)
Subjects: LCSH: Art—Study and teaching. | Material culture. Classification: LCC N87 .B59 2018 | DDC 700.71—dc23
LC record available at https://lccn.loc.gov/2018004216

ISBN 978-0-8077-5919-6 (paper)
ISBN 978-0-8077-7702-2 (ebook)

Printed on acid-free paper
Manufactured in the United States of America

25 24 23 22 21 20 19 18   8 7 6 5 4 3 2 1

To all those who make, use, and aid in the preservation of things.

Contents

Acknowledgments	ix
Introduction	1
Why Material Culture?	2
1. What is Material Culture? Twelve Keys to Understanding Material Culture and This Book	**7**
What Is Material Culture?	8
What Is Not Material Culture?	12
A Confluence Between Material Culture and Art Education	13
Key Ideas for Engaging with This Book	15
Conclusion	25
2. Objects and the Stories of Our Lives	**27**
Approaching Objects	29
Conclusion	37
3. Collecting and Collections	**38**
Objects of Passion	40
Beyond the Visual in Material Culture Studies	42
Collectors and Collecting on the Internet	43
Collecting in the Midst of Catastrophe and Grief	45
Conclusion	48
4. Material Culture: Investigations Spanning Time, People, and Location	**49**
Object Investigation	50

Conclusion	62

5. Technology and Material Culture — 63

A Systems Approach to Technology	66
Technology and Narrative	67
Object Ethnography	68
The Biography of Things	69
The Tetrad	70
The Taxonomy of the Sensorium	71
Videogames and Virtual Environments	73
Conclusion	74

6. Multisensory Art, Artists, and Art Education — 75

Superiority Given the Visual	75
Multisensory Art and Artists	77
Ten Artists/Artistic Teams Whose Work Transcends the Visual	78
Additional Multisensory Artists/Curators, Virtual/Physical Sites, and Events/Exhibitions Readers Are Urged to Explore	84
Multisensory Art and Art Education	85

7. Conclusion: Strategies and Approaches for Teaching About and Studying Material Culture — 87

Ten Instructional Strategies to Use with Students	87
Ten Approaches to Material Culture Study	93

Selected Books Relating to Material Culture, with Interest Toward Art Education	**103**
References	**115**
Index	**121**
About the Authors	**133**

Acknowledgments

We are grateful to Noelle de la Paz, our editor at Teachers College Press, along with Jennifer Baker and Tara Tomczyk, also of Teachers College Press, for their expert and thoughtful guidance in bringing this book to completion. We are grateful for the assistance of Callan Steinmann, Kathryn Farkas (The University of Texas at Austin), and Brianna Hobbs (University of Oregon) for additional editorial assistance.

We are grateful to our students and colleagues at the University of Oregon and The University of Texas at Austin for their insight and responsiveness to our commitment to material culture studies in our research and teaching.

Finally, thank you to our spouses, Linda Beal Blandy and Jane Bolin, for their support and encouragement of our commitment to art education and specifically during the writing of this book.

Introduction

We begin with a battered trunk from Ireland and a small antique ceramic pitcher filled with pennies. Each of these objects is foundational to our appreciation and understanding of the significance of things, and helps motivate us to write this book.

Doug Blandy's maternal grandparents, Waldo and Hazel Johnston, were avid collectors. Hazel collected cut glass and hand-thrown jugs. Waldo collected tools of various types. Both talked with their grandson about their collections as a way to connect him with their childhoods on farms in late-19th-century rural Ohio. Important to their stories was a rough-hewn 21.5- by 40-by 20-inch trunk that contained the possessions of Waldo's Scotch-Irish forebears, immigrants to the United States in the mid-19th century. This trunk, along with their collections of things, connected Doug to his grandparents' past as well as to the historical events that shaped their lives, the life of his mother, and by extension, his own.

At the elementary school Paul Bolin attended in the early 1960s, a half-pint of milk for lunch could be purchased for three cents. Before leaving for school each day, he and his siblings would go to a small old brown ceramic pitcher in the family kitchen and retrieve from it three cents to pay for their milk, with pennies accumulated in pocket change that his parents had gathered throughout the week. The retrieval of these coins for lunch milk each day became a ritual of sustenance; the pennies in the pitcher were also objects of Paul's curiosity. At least once a week, Paul would spread the 50 or so pennies from the pitcher on the floor and search for any coins that were more than a few years old, at the same time wondering about the travel stories each penny would tell if it could. Where had it journeyed, and why? Who handled it, and how was it spent? Because the pennies were silent, Paul used his young imagination to create delightful tales of the coins exciting travel adventures. One day in his search through the milk money, Paul found a penny dated 1913 and minted in San Francisco. This 50-year-old one-cent piece was far older than any coin Paul, as an 8-year-old, had handled, and became a pointed beginning of his serious coin collecting and the object investigation in which he engages today.

Such objects described here were generally not part of the art historical record presented to us as public school students and later at university as preservice art educators. Both of us were uneasy, as learners and educators, by this omission. Why were those things associated directly with our heritage and interests overlooked and ignored in formal education settings? As a consequence, beginning with our doctoral work in the 1980s, we sought alternative approaches to the way history and art history were presented to us. In searching for such alternatives, we discovered the vital and growing area of literature and investigation known as material culture studies, and began to infuse our teaching and research with theory and applications from this field.

WHY MATERIAL CULTURE?

Through the 1980s, the field of art education was very much focused on teaching about the arts from the disciplinary perspective of fine artists, art historians, aestheticians, and art critics. There were outliers to this activity, of course. Art educators like June King McFee and Vincent Lanier at the University of Oregon, and Ron Neperud at the University of Wisconsin–Madison, were preparing art educators to teach about the fine arts, and also to explore the wide and vibrant fields of design, environmental arts, and popular culture in innovative and meaningful ways. However, beginning in the late 1980s, because of both external and internal pressure associated with an increasingly diverse racial and ethnic population in the United States, social justice advocates, emerging technologies, the increasing importance of design, as well as emerging multidisciplinary and transdisciplinary orientations within higher education, the content of the field began to broaden and change in earnest. Theoretical viewpoints and approaches from the fields of anthropology, folklore, sociology, history, popular culture, philosophy, and political science, among others, began to be integrated into research and teaching within art education. Visual culture became an attractive theoretical orientation within art education because of its interdisciplinarity. The emergence of visual culture was an important first step in broadening the theoretical and practical focus of art education; however, even a visual culture orientation is too narrowly focused to capture the plethora of multimedia and multisensory forms that learners of all ages are actively engaging today.

Investigations and literature found within the field of material culture studies contributes to an evolving pedagogy about the meaning of "things" in the lives of children, youth, and adults. The chapters that follow address theory and practice related to critically engaging a wide range of historical and contemporary things referred to as material culture.

The term *material culture* can be found in academic writings about objects and their meanings as early as 1875 (Schlereth, 1985, 1992).

Since that time, material culture has taken on a variety of connotations and undergone a number of nuanced changes in meaning and application. Our position is that material culture is "a descriptor of any and all human-constructed or human-mediated objects, forms, or expressions, manifested consciously or unconsciously through culturally acquired behaviors" (Bolin & Blandy, 2003, p. 249).

In the seven chapters that follow, we explore myriad topics and issues that inform a material culture studies orientation to art education. Readers will also discover in these chapters the relevance of teaching about material culture in fields of study such as history, social studies, language arts, art history, and communications, among others.

Chapter 1, "What Is Material Culture? Twelve Keys to Understanding Material Culture and This Book," provides readers with an orientation to the field of material culture studies. Twelve key ideas for understanding this book and material culture studies are introduced and discussed, enabling readers to gain a fundamental acquaintance with material culture studies and its relationship to the field of art education. The twelve key ideas are as follows:

- Distinguishing the term *material culture* from *material culture studies*
- Acknowledging the interdisciplinary nature of material culture studies
- Recognizing the value of story in the exploration of material culture
- Apprehending the political nature of material culture
- Considering the role of memory (individual and collective) in the study of material culture
- Respecting the significance of collecting and collections
- Perceiving connections between material culture and the human senses
- Noting differences and similarities between the fields of material culture studies and visual culture
- Understanding the importance of both making and responding to objects and spaces
- Employing metaphoric approaches to the study of material culture
- Supporting the value of studying tangible objects
- Exploring a variety of approaches to the study of material culture

In Chapter 2, "Objects and the Stories of Our Lives," we explore the intertwined relationships between objects and stories in the lives of people. Some questions addressed in this chapter include: What objects do people possess and hold dear? Why is this so? How do an object and the stories that surround it work together to enhance the meaning and value of both object and story? Is the value of an object measured only monetarily? What else might come into play to determine an object's worth? In addressing these questions, this chapter describes a number of activities and approaches we have used with our students to investigate the dynamic relationships that can emerge through sharing stories about objects in our lives.

In Chapter 3, "Collecting and Collections," we investigate the role that collections and collecting play in the lives of people. Through discussions of past and current collectors and collections, whether these are Barbie dolls, kitchen magnets, or works of fine art, we address the apparently vital human and cross-cultural experience of collecting objects and possessing collections.

In Chapter 4, "Material Culture: Investigations Spanning Time, People, and Location," two specific objects are examined. These items are presented to illustrate the benefit of object study and to exemplify how objects may be explored across time, people's experience, and physical location. These discussions are included to spark and motivate educators in a variety of contexts to engage learners in hands-on object-directed learning. The first of these two objects is a child's rocking chair, a family heirloom that has been in Paul Bolin's family for more than 110 years. Here, family history is explored through the use of text and photographs. The second object of study discussed in this chapter is an animated book, available through a website, of a traditional Chinese folktale. The narrative provides the opportunity to consider (and perhaps reconsider) the often partisan and sometimes even bigoted notions that emerge when denoting the meaning and merit of unfamiliar things, ideas and, more important, the people associated with them.

Chapter 5, "Technology and Material Culture," introduces readers to the important position of technology within the history of material culture. Material culture studies and related fields have much to offer in the investigation and critical examination of technology, including those technologies emerging today. Discussion and investigative approaches introduced in this chapter are included to promote an understanding of the critical transparency necessary to educate people about the complex and interwoven relationships present among technology, society, and culture. Specific examples show how technology may be explored critically.

In Chapter 6, "Multisensory Art, Artists, and Art Education," we confront the privileged place sight has been given within our world—including the art world—today. Sight is often regarded as being of greater value than the senses of touch, hearing, taste, and smell; this affects how we engage and prioritize material and "visual" culture. However, this hierarchical positioning of the senses is being challenged within the world of contemporary art, as a growing number of artists work with senses other than sight. In this chapter, we discuss the work of 12 individuals, or teams, whose artistic endeavors transcend the visual. These artists include Edward Kienholz, Bridget Baker, Tony Oursler, and Kate Goodwin, among others. Additionally, we provide a list of 25 multisensory artists and curators, virtual or physical sites about multisensory art, and multisensory art events and exhibitions to explore online or in person.

In the conclusion, Chapter 7, "Strategies and Approaches for Teaching About and Studying Material Culture," we describe various instructional activities that the authors have used successfully with a wide range of students (K–16) and in diverse learning contexts (schools, museums, community locations). Moreover, this chapter also contains descriptions of 10 approaches to the study of material culture we have gleaned from writers in various fields such as art history, anthropology, museum studies, material culture studies, and environmental aesthetics. In presenting these activities and approaches for engaging in the study of material culture, our intent is to build on the ideas presented and provide learners of all ages with motivation and direction for exploring a wide range of material culture within our world today.

We conclude this volume with an extensive bibliography of books about material culture, with particular interest to the field of art education. This book list is included to encourage readers to explore the vast and expanding body of resources within and related to the field of material culture studies.

Our hope is for this book to be a source of inspiration, informational resource, instructional guide, and motivational catalyst for preservice educators, teachers, and scholars, associated with a variety of educational environments to use pedagogical strategies leading to critical engagements with objects. We invite readers to join us in carrying out a rich and meaningful discussion about the significance of objects in the lives of others as well as ourselves.

CHAPTER 1

What Is Material Culture?
Twelve Keys to Understanding Material Culture and This Book

Objects and spaces that surround us each day are commonly referred to as *material culture*. This two-word term encompasses the vast variety of artifacts and human-formed environments that society as a whole and specific individuals deem important to their lives. Material culture is generally regarded to comprise the purposefully constructed or intentionally acquired things we encounter, as well as the human-made spaces within our world. The subject of material culture is quite broad and encompasses a full range of objects and spaces in the past and present, yet discussions of material culture in this volume center primarily on objects. These are the items that help imbue our everyday lives with experience and meaning, the things and spaces that have been designed, shaped, fabricated, constructed, assembled, altered, devised, manufactured, or produced through some form of human activity. Material culture, then, is a reference to the human-formed objects, spaces, and expressions that make up our world, and frequently includes the articles we construct and/or possess for the purpose of personal memory making and the shaping of individual or group identity.

The term *material culture* has been in use for over 140 years to describe the objects and spaces that make up our world (Schlereth, 1985, 1992). During this time, the term *material culture* has been defined in a wide range of ways, yet most writers about material culture center their ideas on a belief that fundamental yet sometimes veiled relationships occur between people and the objects and spaces they encounter. To perceive and understand the valuable but frequently unrecognized connections that exist between people and objects or spaces requires thoughtful exploration and analysis. It is our belief that in order to secure a comprehensive understanding of the objects and constructed spaces that form our world, we must investigate and understand in deep and rich ways the people who make and use these objects and spaces. Conversely, in order to comprehend thoughtfully the vast spectrum of people that inhabit our world, it is to our advantage if we investigate thoroughly the myriad objects and spaces that these individuals and groups create, use, respond to, and in some ways, preserve. As Sheumaker and Wajda (2008) state succinctly, the engagement of studying material culture "has been, and remains, to expand the understanding of human existence through attention to the relationships between objects and people" (p. xii). Because people make and shape things and spaces, and these fabricated objects and environments, in turn, help make to shape and influence individuals in the surrounding world, it is valuable for people to recognize and explore the important reciprocal relationships that occur between ourselves and the multitude of things and constructed spaces that form the world around us.

WHAT IS MATERIAL CULTURE?

Getting a handle on the term *material culture* is not as easy as it may seem at first. For some people, *material culture* describes objects uncovered from centuries and millennia past, a designation given to artifacts unearthed while sifting through the matter of some faraway time and territory and is more tied to archaeological investigations than to items within our contemporary world. Although this may be the case for some objects, it is not so for all. Objects of material culture can be those we collect in our homes; carry with us in backpacks, purses, and pockets; and stow on shelves in the back of closets—often, the things we should discard even if we cannot bring ourselves to do so. Material culture also describes the articles we proudly display in our lives—photos, artworks, and handcrafted objects; memorabilia from past trips; and markers of time and life's adventures and accomplishments. The term *material culture* delineates the entire array of human-formed objects and spaces in our world. These items become tangible reminders of the many stories—both told and unspoken—that constitute our lives.

One useful way to apprehend what is meant by *material culture* is to add a grammatical preposition and article between the two words that make up this designation, so that it becomes the "material *of a* culture." In this way, such expressions become the physical and sensory manifestations that people make, use, respond to, and preserve within their world. Material culture denotes the constructed things and spaces around us, and thus items of material culture become important in helping us understand the values, beliefs, thoughts, skills, qualities, actions, and attributes of the people involved with them. Tilley, Keane, Küchler, Rowlands, and Spyer (2006) call the investigation of material culture an analysis of "things as material matter, as found or made, as static or mobile, rare or ubiquitous, local or exotic, new or old, ordinary or special, small or monumental, traditional or modern, simple or complex" (p. 4). These authors go on to state that the study of such objects explores "the manner in which people think through themselves, and their lives and identities through the medium of different kinds of things" (p. 4). The study of material culture involves a look at both people and things, and the consequential interconnection that occurs between them.

Working from this idea, the terrain of what encompasses material culture seems quite vast. And so it is. Ian Woodward (2007) has referred to the wide purview of material culture in this way:

> In its popular scholarly usage, the term "material culture" is generally taken to refer to any material object (e.g., shoes, cup, pen) or network of material objects (e.g., house, car, shopping mall) that people perceive, touch, use and handle, carry out social activities within, use or contemplate. (p. 14)

Thus, the breadth of objects designated "material culture" is significantly far ranging. And so is the study of individuals and groups who come to bear on these objects and spaces as shapers and/or users of these items (see Figure 1.1). Reinforcing this idea, Sheumaker and Wajda (2008) have captured the broad expanse of material culture, and the study of it, quite well:

> *Material culture* encompasses those things that have physical form and presence, whether an object you can hold in your hand; an environment in which you live, work, worship, or play; or an image of the landscape you captured with your digital camera as you traversed a pond or a mountain range. Material culture is, then, culture made material—that is, it is the physical manifestations of human endeavor, of minds at work (and play), of social, economic, and political processes affecting all of us. (p. xi)

Material culture denotes those purposeful things and spaces that bring meaning, joy, knowledge, expression, contemplation, experience, and wonderment to our lives. They range from small in size—perhaps a coin, a needle, or a personal sitting area—to those items large in physical scope: an automobile, a house, place of worship, or even an entire cityscape (see Figure 1.2).

Material culture encompasses those artifacts and locations whose monetary and social value is agreed upon and readily apparent, such as a work of fine art or piece of noted historical memorabilia. It also includes those items whose significance is more personal and perhaps obscure, such as a collectible kitchen magnet, a well-used softball glove, or an inexpensive but cherished gift from a friend or family member (see Figure 1.3).

Figure 1.1. Students exploring an animal pelt.

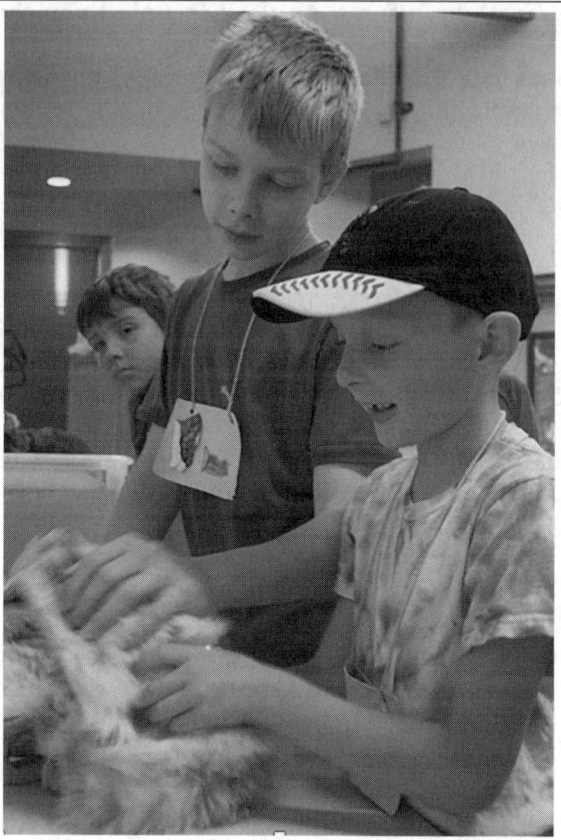

Photograph courtesy of the University of Oregon Museum of Natural and Cultural History

Many of us are surrounded by a multitude of things. Some of these items are easily viewed as significant to our lives, such as photographs of family and friends, elegant jewelry, works of art, electronic communication devices, and other expensive objects of everyday experience. The importance of these items is readily recognized, as they are the things we frequently choose to keep close at hand, hold in esteem, or interact with on a regular basis. Although it is not always the case, many of these special objects are acknowledged to be of worth and import because of the highly valued place these treasured articles occupy within society as a whole. The agreed-upon appraisal of these artifacts is established and reinforced through cultural and social beliefs manifested by ourselves and by those around us.

The meaningfulness of other objects we possess is more hidden. The value of these items is often concealed from view and generally

Figure 1.2. Students experiencing the gold-tiled dome in the Prince Lucien Campbell Courtyard of the University of Oregon Jordan Schnitzer Museum of Art.

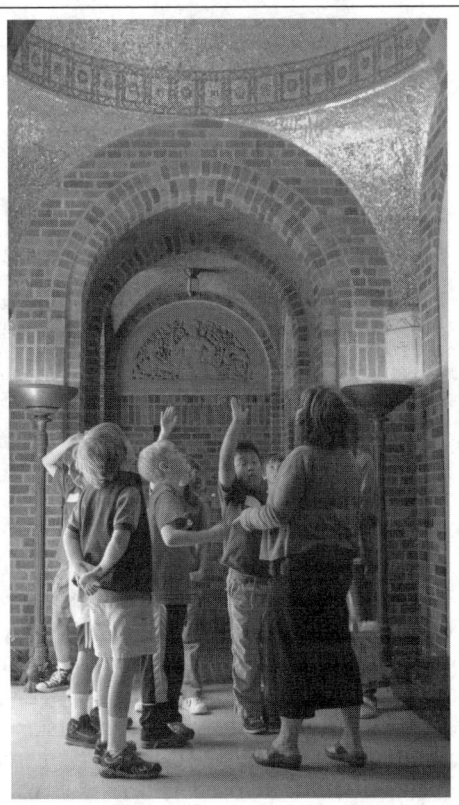

Photograph courtesy of the Jordan Schnitzer Museum of Art

goes beyond a dollars-and-cents assessment. The significance of these objects resides not in their monetary worth but in the personal value that these articles hold for their possessor. Many of us decide to retain certain things in our lives because of the importance we believe these items have for us individually. We choose to hold on to particular things because of what these items mean to us; however, the worth of these objects for others is often not readily apparent, and it may even be difficult for them to discern or to acknowledge that these objects hold any value at all.

Perhaps we desire to keep in our possession a memento given to us that marks a notable life occasion. Or maybe we seek out some relatively inexpensive object purchased or found and brought back from a trip or family vacation to refresh our memory of this special event at some later time. We may choose to keep a particular item as a tangible token/reminder of a significant experience or place that we, with our frail

Figure 1.3. Image of a softball glove.

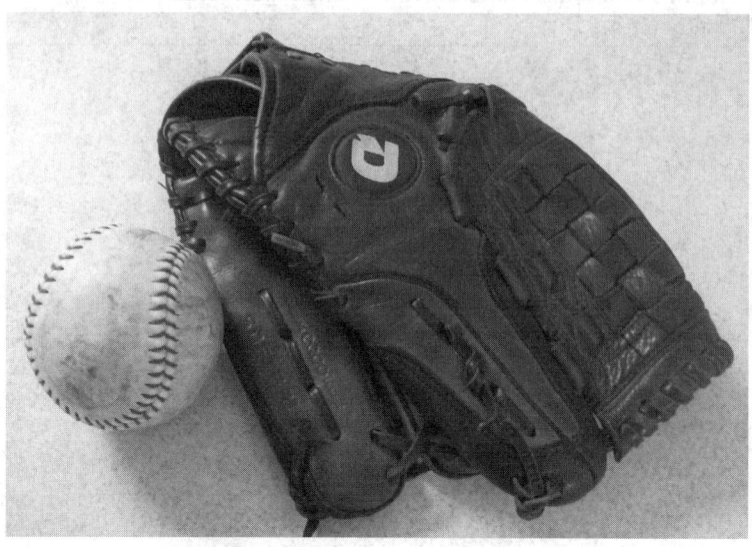

Photograph courtesy of Paul Bolin

human memory, do not want to forget. This specific article becomes a material objectification of something, someplace, or someone we have encountered in another time or location, and kept and cherished for the purpose of retaining the memory or attempting to grasp a fleeting fragment of that important life experience. Some objects are kept in an effort to help recall a memory associated with the actual item. Such specific "special-ized" objects kept in our possession assist us in distinguishing who we have been, who we are at the present time, and perhaps who we would like to become someday.

WHAT IS NOT MATERIAL CULTURE?

Material culture encompasses a wide territory of objects, spaces, and expressions. Yet even in this expansive breadth, material culture is not a linguistic designation that "includes a totally unrestricted spectrum of all possible objects" (Schlereth, 1985, p. 5). What distinguishes *all possible objects* from being considered material culture is the presence of purposeful human agency or human activity in the formation or use of material culture. Things that reside outside the realm of what is shaped by human intervention are generally considered *not* to be material culture. Expounding on this idea, Schlereth (1985) has stated that "natural objects such as trees, fossils, or skeletons are usually excluded from definitions of material culture on the grounds that they are not [hu]man-made or [hu]man-modified artifacts" (p. 5). Worthwhile and scintillating arguments abound regarding whether *any* object or space is truly isolated from at least some degree of human intervention within our highly complex and systemically connected world today, yet it is most useful for gaining an initial grasp of the delineation of material culture to consider things such as naturally deposited rocks, arbitrarily growing trees, and randomly situated seashells on an ocean beach examples of those items that reside outside what is most often considered material culture. Thus, material culture is designated as such because of the impact of human engagement on shaping these objects and spaces, thereby differentiating naturally formed and situated things in the world from human-mediated artifacts and spaces.

A CONFLUENCE BETWEEN MATERIAL CULTURE AND ART EDUCATION

The subject of art has had an active presence in public schools and other formal educational environments in the United States for nearly 200 years. It should be noted, however, that throughout this span of time, the study of art, especially within the public schools, has been rife with contention. There have been many—and often conflicting—purposes voiced regarding the teaching of art in public schools, including art instruction intended to build moral citizens, increase vocational possibilities, teach elements and principles of design, express creative thinking, and assist students in becoming knowledgeable consumers. There have even been times when art was taught in the United States for the stated purpose of strengthening national security. Over the years, instruction and learning in art has been about many things. Bolin and Hoskings (2015) compiled a list showing 50 different purposes for teaching art in schools and other sites in which art education occurs.

A focus that undergirds much of this contentious discussion about art education centers on various notions of what is meant by "art." If someone believes that the world of art is fairly limited in scope, perhaps encompassing primarily those things purposely intended for art museums and displayed therein, then that person's view of art education will likely reflect a similarly narrowed sensibility. If someone else believes art includes a wider terrain of objects and spaces, then that individual's acknowledged purposes for teaching about these artifacts is apt to increase concurrently, thus fueling a subsequent conflict between the two different people, with their diverse views of art and art education. Such differences regarding how art and art education are viewed and carried out in practice have produced a longstanding legacy of contention for art education. How one sees art will affect how that person regards art education; how one perceives art education will determine how he or she teaches art.

There exist a tremendous number of objects in the world that are considered art, even among those with a somewhat constrained view of what is contained within the disciplined territory of this field. However, if one accepts the broad-based position of W. David Kingery (1996) that "all objects are to some extent art and thus require consideration of both form and content" (p. 14), then strong alignment occurs between objects thought to be art and those considered material culture. Under these circumstances, there is little difference recognized between art and material culture. Art is not seen as one thing and material culture another; it is here that the worlds of art, art education, and material culture coalesce. Noted art educator June King McFee, writing as early as 1970, offered striking similarities between art and material culture:

> Art is that form of human behavior by which man [or woman] purposefully interprets and enhances the quality or essence of experience through the things he [or she] produces—from the simple enhancement of a tool to the expression of his [or her] deepest feelings and profound projections in painting, sculpture, architecture, and city planning. (p. 30)

To June McFee and other art educators with analogous perspectives, there is little difference between objects and spaces designated as art, and those termed *material culture.*

Art educators who dismiss the appropriateness of aligning the investigation of material culture with the study of art appear to purposely or unknowingly express a narrowly determined sensibility about the purview of art. Our view on the subject differs from that held by these individuals, and is more in line with that proposed by Irving Lavin (1983), who wrote:

> The first assumption is that anything [hu]man-made is a work of art, even the lowliest and most purely functional object. Man[/Woman], indeed, might be defined as the art-making animal, and the fact that we choose to regard only some [hu]man-made things as works of art is a matter of conditioning. (p. 98)

Sadly, from our perspective, this "matter of conditioning" in limiting people's view regarding the range of what may be considered art is often an outcome of the formal art instruction delivered to our students. Too frequently, students in our classrooms and other locations of art education are exposed only to those objects and spaces that have been traditionally regarded as "fine art" or "high art," works that have made their way into the renowned art museums and exhibition halls of the world.

For this reason, students emerge from these learning environments with a reified view of art being situated within a tightly bordered parameter of the gilded frame or set elevated on a stark white pedestal. Through this "matter of conditioning," students learn to recognize those objects considered highly prized and worthy of study. The purposefully designed objects and spaces—those items of material culture that are often situated within the immediate surroundings of our students—are frequently omitted from acknowledgment and study within our art classrooms, and thus are not even apparent within the students' knowledge base of possible consideration and thoughtful investigation. Teacher choices of what to include in the art curriculum may often constrict student explorations within the wide world of material culture.

Art education is a field with tremendous potential to expand our students' sensibilities about art and its role within the world. If we as art educators do not take this upon ourselves, who will? This expansion of the role that art plays in students' lives will take place only through purposeful and decisive action by those of us actively involved in art education. We believe art educators must seize this opportunity to expand the possibilities of their field and enlarge its impact within the world today. The study of material culture is likely not the single feature that will solve all problems within art education. However, we do believe that by providing our students with increased attention to things and spaces around us in the world—the material culture of our lives—the study of art can indeed have a much richer and immediate impact on their lives.

KEY IDEAS FOR ENGAGING WITH THIS BOOK

We offer 12 key ideas to assist readers to further their understanding of material culture and art education and how we treat these subjects in this book. Woven throughout the following chapters, specifically in Chapter 7, are an abundance of teaching and learning approaches and activities for students—some brief and some extended examples—whose purpose and value become more useful after reading the discussions for each of the following key ideas. These descriptive sections are included to help give ideational grounding and make more meaningful the practical teaching and learning opportunities offered throughout the book. *Please do not skip or skim over this material.* Your engagement with this book and with the exploration of material culture in art education will be enhanced significantly through the brief discussions that follow. These 12 considerations about material culture become important keys for unlocking the greatest benefit from the ideas, activities, and instructional approaches for exploring human-formed objects and spaces presented throughout the pages of this book.

Key Idea 1: Distinguishing the Term Material Culture from Material Culture Studies

The term *material culture* has been used frequently in two ways. First, it is utilized as a descriptor of the entire breadth of human made or modified objects, forms, spaces, and expressions. It denotes the full spectrum of artifacts, past and present, that are encountered within the nearby world or drawn from distant locations. Second, the term *material culture* is used to describe the gamut of investigative methods, approaches, and activities in which cultural inquiry is employed to scrutinize these human-formed and modified objects and spaces firsthand. This duality of meaning for material culture has at times obscured a clear and specific denotation of the term, thus creating some confusion in cases where "material culture stands for both the subject to be researched as well as the method of studying the subject" (Schlereth, 1985, p. 6).

To overcome this ambiguity and to make clear the distinction of how the term is used in any particular situation, researchers in various fields now employ the separate terms *material culture* and *material culture studies* to describe features of their work. *Material culture* is used to reference the artifacts and other human-mediated forms and expressions in the world, while *material culture studies* describes the efforts and processes undertaken to investigate and interpret these various forms of material culture. For this reason, the term *material cultural studies* is used "to describe the research, writing, teaching, exhibiting, and publishing of individuals who endeavor to interpret past and present human activity . . . through extant physical evidence" (Schlereth, 1985, p. 6). Throughout the exploration of human-constructed objects and spaces, it is useful to recognize the linguistic distinction drawn between the specific thing or mediated space being studied (material culture), and the process or approach undertaken in the investigation of these objects and spaces (material culture studies).

Key Idea 2: Acknowledging the Interdisciplinary Nature of Material Culture Studies

Objects and spaces form an integral part of the lives of people throughout the world. For this reason, the field of material culture studies has pertinence for and connection with a multitude of individuals and subject areas. Material culture studies is not an isolated field; it is by nature a process of investigating territory that is increasingly recognized to touch the experiences and actions of people in far-ranging regions of the physical, social, psychological, religious, and intellectual landscape. Without question, an extensive number of individuals and groups is experiencing the investigation of objects and constructed spaces as useful in their work. Martin and Garrison (1997) submit that "there is hardly a field or profession where the study of material evidence has not raised new questions or brought new insights to old ones" (p. 403), whereas W. J. T. Mitchell (2005) notes a recent "eruption of interest in material culture in academia" (p. 111).

A look into the multitude of literature directed toward the investigation of material culture displays an expanding list of subject areas that are becoming vitally engaged in the study of tangible objects and spaces. These fields include, but are not limited to, advertising, aesthetics, African American studies, anthropology, archaeology, architecture, art, art education, art history, biology, civic planning, cultural studies, design, economics, education and schooling, fashion, folklore, food and foodways, gender studies, geography, graphic design, hermeneutics, historic preservation, history, horticulture, industrial archaeology, genetics, landscape architecture, law, library science, materials conservation, materials science research, microphysics, museum studies, numismatics, philosophy, political science, popular culture, psychoanalysis, psychology, religious studies, semiotics, sociology, technology, and textile studies. Art education is only one of many subject fields beginning to investigate and learn from those participating in the field of material culture studies. The list of subject areas engaged in the utilization and investigation of material culture extends onward, and will surely increase as the number and variety of human-shaped objects and spaces in our world continues to expand.

Because of this growth in a multidisciplined approach to the investigation of objects and spaces, Knappett (2005) sees this as "an exciting time to be thinking through material culture and its central yet ambiguous role in human societies" (p. 2). It is exhilarating to see the burgeoning activity of material culture studies within a growing variety of disciplines, and concurrently important to acknowledge that this disciplinary expansion and crossover will likely require increased conversation, engaged collaboration, and at times, thoughtful negotiation among participants and researchers in various fields in order to reap the most benefit from these future explorations. Such multidisciplined participatory associations will likely require new ways of thinking about art education and inspire changes in how we conduct our efforts in this field.

Key Idea 3: Recognizing the Value of Story in the Exploration of Material Culture

Our lives are shaped by a myriad of stories drawn from our past and present experience. Some of these personal narratives are meant to be told; others, we believe, are tales probably best kept to ourselves. Either way, the act of engaging with and reflecting on the stories of our lives helps form a sense of who we have been, who we are now, and perhaps who we would like to become someday. When considered deeply, many of these stories concern our experience with objects and constructed spaces encountered either in our hazy, distant past or in times much clearer and closer to the present. Whether they are stories about objects of material culture drawn from our childhood, remembrances of playing or working with particular items from our world during our adolescent years, tales of the special things we used and spaces inhabited as we developed as adults, or recollections of memorable objects and eventful spaces held on to as we grow old, these retrospective experiences frequently occur by way of connecting our memory stories alongside our previous encounters with particular objects.

In and of themselves, things are things and spaces are spaces. Objects and constructed environments are not awarded a noteworthy position in the world writ large or in our personal lives, apart from the status we and others bestow on them. Objects and mediated spaces become either special or overlooked primarily because we chose to position them in these ways, and such placement by us and others occurs often through an infusion or lack of story. Therefore, to explore these objects and spaces in meaningful ways requires an investigation of the often rich and multilayered stories that surround them.

Key Idea 4: Apprehending the Political Nature of Material Culture

Objects and constructed spaces are not neutral dispassionate artifacts situated in life today or gleaned from a more or less distant past. Acknowledged or not, all items of material culture are carriers of human expression as well as possible initiators of human response. Material culture reflects purposeful expressive activity carried out by one or more individuals, which calls for some form of sensory reaction. Thus, all objects and spaces are in some way involved with people through the processes by which these objects and spaces are responded to and created. These creations and modifications carry with them, as well as reveal, values, beliefs, actions, and characteristics of their makers that can be evident, obscure, or some combination of the two.

In some cases, the political disposition of objects and spaces is clearly recognizable and intentional, as in the case of election buttons, candidate posters, campaign television commercials, civil disobedience ephemera, political party symbols, and encounters with structures such as the Statue of Liberty or the massive sculptural representations of four U.S. presidents on the face of Mount Rushmore. The political intent of these objects and structures is quite evident. There are other times, however, when the political character of objects and spaces is not so readily apparent, but is still powerful. This more hidden political presence may be found, for example, in the colors and design of clothing worn by members of a specific gang, group, or sports team; in structures and spaces constructed in ways that succeed or fail to accommodate and assist people with a range of physical or psychological needs; and also in objects manufactured, without full disclosure, utilizing nonrenewable and nonrecyclable materials. We must recognize that all objects around us are produced in a systemically connected, politically functioning world that is shaped by the values, beliefs, and attitudes of those who make, respond to, and use these objects and spaces. The study of material culture must involve the exploration and analysis of objects and constructed spaces in ways that are deep, complex, and meaningful, both individually and socially. It is to our advantage and that of our students to recognize the political nature of the mediated objects and spaces that surround us each day.

Key Idea 5: Regarding the Role of Memory (Individual and Collective) in the Study of Material Culture

Most of us are forgetful. As hard as we may try and as good as some are at recalling the detail and vibrancy of life experiences, most of what we encounter and consider on a daily basis easily slips into the world of the forgotten. This is especially true regarding the rich sensory experiences that make up our lives: Pungent smells, vivid feelings, resonant sounds, and intense tastes we encounter in the surrounding world may quickly lose their graphic presence as we carry out our daily business. For this reason, objects are often utilized by individuals and groups to help remember those special life experiences that they wish to hold on to. These tangible items secured in the past help define and position us in the world today, and assist us in negotiating life between the world of the past and that of the present.

Objects of material culture can be used to situate and give substance to memories that are easily forgotten. This retention of memory may occur through photos we take of people and places visited, found natural or human-made items that we collect and bring back from specific locations of travel, items of purchase that help us recall memorable experiences firsthand, or gifts presented to us that mark special occasions in life. The objects received, collected, and retained in this way become objectified reminders that assist in giving substance to memory and help us hold on to particular meaningful life experiences we have encountered in earlier times and other places.

Key Idea 6: Respecting the Significance of Collecting and Collections

People throughout the world, including many of our students, are collectors. There is a vast array of objects that people collect: Their assemblages may be comprised of things such as kitchen magnets, T-shirts, teaspoons, stamps or coins, action figures, certain types of jewelry, stuffed animals, coffee mugs, or even tattoos (depending on the age of the collector). There are many reasons why people collect things, and these reasons raise intriguing questions about the activity of collecting: What motivates a person to collect objects? Why are some people collectors and others not? What is the difference between collecting objects and possessing a collection? In what ways is the practice of *collecting* things similar to and different from *gathering* things? When does collecting become hoarding? Why do a large number of children between the ages of about 8 and 13 actively engage in collecting? Do people who collect things as adults begin collecting when they were children? Why do some people hide their collections while others display them? What signifies the worth of an object and a collection—is its value monetary, intrinsic, or to some degree both? What, besides tangible things, may be collected?

To explore these and other worthwhile questions related to collections and collecting requires a multilayered investigation of people and their relationship with things—an examination of a person's relationship with not only a single item, but with multiple objects that are brought together to form a collection. Because material culture studies centers on analyses of interrelated connections between people and things, its ideas, literature, and research approaches to material culture are extremely useful for the study of collections, collectors, and the activity of collecting.

Key Idea 7: Perceiving Connections Between Material Culture and the Human Senses

Material culture, as defined broadly within the field of material culture studies and related fields, as well as for the purposes of this book, consists of "any and all human constructed or human-mediated objects, forms, or expressions, manifested consciously or unconsciously through culturally acquired behaviors" (Bolin & Blandy, 2003, p. 249). As such, any singular or collective example of material culture may be created and experienced through hearing, touching, tasting, smelling, or seeing. This is not to imply that any particular example is created to be experienced equally or primarily through all the senses, but to acknowledge that any given item of material culture may appeal to more than one sense. The interrelationships associated with this sensory appeal are intriguing foci for study.

One might assume that in the field of art education, most of the objects, forms, or expressions that educators and students consider will be primarily visual. This book challenges this assumption by asking educators and learners to recognize and study the multisensory elements that exist not only in constructed forms and expressions that are intended to be encountered through multiple senses, but also around objects or spaces created to be experienced visually. For example, whereas it may be possible for a museum visitor to experience any given example of visual art on exhibit primarily through sight, to do so the visitor may ignore other features of the museum experience. These may include the feel of spatial qualities and ambiance of the gallery in which the work is located, the juxtaposition of the work in relationship to other works on display, the smells associated with other visitors to the exhibition and the influence of these aromas on how the art is perceived, and the play of sound from the movement and conversations of others in the gallery contributing to the larger political and sociocultural context associated with encountering the work.

Multisensory influences associated with art and design are becoming increasingly abundant. Consider the work of Markus J. Buehler, a materials scientist at the Massachusetts Institute of Technology (MIT), who is translating the sequences of amino acids spun into silk fibers as musical compositions. These compositions are then analyzed for qualities that equate to better silk fibers. (An extensive discussion and bibliography associated with Buehler's Laboratory for Atomistic and Molecular Mechanics can be found at web.mit.edu/mbuchler/www/.) This example has particular relevance, as instances of what is referred to as BioArt proliferate and are selected for inclusion within art education curricula. Such an illustration of multisensory art is also relevant as art education continues to embrace design as a curricular focus.

Key Idea 8: Noting Differences and Similarities Between the Fields of Material Culture Studies and Visual Culture

Both material culture and visual culture are associated with academic fields that view materiality or visuality as a source of study within a cultural context. Material culture studies and visual culture are interdisciplinary fields and are strongly connected to each other as well as to other academic areas associated with the study of culture. Such fields include, but are not limited to, anthropology, art history, cultural studies, ethnomusicology, folklore, media studies, and sensory studies. In turn, several theoretical perspectives associated with critical theory, literary theory, feminist theory, race theory, social theory, political theory, performance studies, media theory, education studies, communication studies, and art education inform the fields of material culture studies and visual culture.

In our view, the study of material culture and visual culture are complementary and mutually informative. One may begin with either perspective and then expand outward to a material culture studies approach, or focus in through a visual culture approach. The primary difference between the two fields is the multisensory orientation of material culture studies and the primary focus on visuality inherent to visual culture. (To see how this focus manifests itself, consider Evans & Hall, 1999; Freedman, 2003; Mirzoeff, 2009, 2012; Sturken & Cartwright, 2001.) As a consequence, the literature of each field, though mutually informative, is not duplicative. Whereas similarities exist between the two fields, as described above, the current body of literature within visual culture, because of its primary focus on the visual, does not address the range of topics, ideas, objects, and research methodologies examined and utilized within material culture studies.

It is also important to note that an emphasis on visual culture may exclude those students who experience visual impairments. Emphasizing material culture encourages the use of multisensory examples, thus accommodating the needs of students with various types of sensory impairments by offering alternatives.

Key Idea 9: Understanding the Importance of Both Making and Responding to Objects and Spaces

Over many years, art education has been a field primarily involved with making things. The wide array of books, journal articles, curriculum guides, and other theoretical and instructional resources in art education quite often emphasize the production of art. There are, however, other art education resources and approaches directed toward the analysis and interpretation of existing artworks. This is an important reflective dimension of art education and one that must not be ignored for its power to help expand learners' ideas about art. This dual purpose of art education—both making and responding to art—is one of the compelling links this field has with the study of material culture. Although material culture studies is frequently regarded as a field associated with the investigation of objects and spaces that have already been produced, it is also filled with connections to the study of makers and processes of making. There are times when the actual making of an object provides unique insight into our understanding of an object and its maker, and studying a finished product may reveal information about the creator and the process of how and why the object was made.

One of our primary beliefs about art education aligns this field quite well with material culture studies, and involves the notion of *making* within art education. The study of material culture encourages delving into the processes of both making things and responding to objects and spaces that are already made. Doing so compels us to take on these tasks for the purpose of attempting to *make* meaningful life understandings from making things ourselves and from studying things made by others.

Key Idea 10: Discerning Metaphoric Approaches to the Study of Material Culture

When considering objects and human-formed spaces in our world, we often find it useful to utilize metaphoric analyses with our students. We ask students to draw associations between an object or space and something else that seems immediately unlike and quite removed. How might a paintbrush be like a space capsule? In what ways is the Statue of Liberty similar to a trip to the beach? How is an art museum like a head of lettuce? Such action helps stretch students' involvement and speculation about objects and spaces, challenging them to contemplate and speculate deeply beyond considering the face-to-face superficial exterior of an object or constructed space. In keeping with this idea of metaphoric consideration, we believe that a beneficial outcome of studying material culture occurs through engaging all items of material culture through two, and perhaps three, metaphors: windows, mirrors, and, when appropriate, doorways.

First, the examination of an object or delineated space by way of a metaphoric window enables the investigator to consider this item as a portal through which to peer into another place and time. Such an encounter provides an opportunity for an individual to project into and explore the world of the object, asking why and for what purpose it was initially fashioned: What materials were employed and why? Who was its maker? Who may have been its users? Why has it survived? Has it undergone any alteration over time, and why might this have been so? By considering the object as a window to the past, students are positioned to see beyond themselves and regard and scrutinize the object as a reflection of the time and place wherein it was produced.

A second consideration toward an object or designed space encourages the individual to treat a particular item of material culture as a metaphoric mirror. In this case, the object or space under consideration provides the impetus for us to reflect back on ourselves and wonder about this object in relation to ideas and circumstances today: What does this object reveal not only about the conditions surrounding when it was made, but also its place in our lives now? Have its meaning and cultural and social significance changed over time? If so, why has this shift occurred? Are its use and meaning different now from how it was employed and considered in other times and places? What might an exploration of this object reveal about the values and beliefs of people today, including our own? Exploring the purpose, use, significance, and meaning of an object or space through the metaphoric ideas of both windows and mirrors provides an avenue toward reaching a rich and deep awareness of the object or space, enabling us to peer into a time apart from our own, as well as consider thoughtfully our place in the world today.

A third metaphoric consideration of an object or space may occur by way of an actual sensory encounter, of touch, smell, sound, or taste. In this case, the utilization of a metaphoric doorway may be useful. Beyond a window or mirror, which are both sight-based, a doorway is a location that permits physical entrance. A doorway provides the person with experiences that are multisensory in nature. The study of material culture encourages investigation of specific objects, spaces, or expressions that can sometimes be contacted directly through the senses of touch, sound, taste, or smell. When possible, learners should be permitted and encouraged to do so. In this situation, the encounters with material culture occur firsthand and are approached through the metaphoric doorway that enables direct contact and physical exploration, providing new dimensions for deeper insight and richer understanding.

Key Idea 11: Supporting the Value of Studying Tangible Objects

An increasing amount of life and learning that people experience each day occurs through a two-dimensional screen. Much of our world is apprehended by means of an escalating range of mediated digital technology, and thus becomes an abstraction often well removed from the actual experience, event, person, object, or topic of concern. Information available to us, although often vibrantly overwhelming in amount, spectrum of content, and accessibility, is presented to us via a somewhat limited format. As a result, much of what we learn and know comes by way of a flat, two-dimensional surface of pixels, sometimes augmented with corresponding sound.

The study of material culture provides another approach to information acquisition and learning. It is based, whenever possible, on direct and immediate contact with actual objects and spaces, and involves exploration into these objects and locations as tangible and material information. There is much to be teased out and learned by investigating them. Our engagements with such objects and spaces may also transcend visual encounters, and embrace a wide range of the senses. Objects and spaces may be visited, touched, smelled, listened to, and even tasted in ways that current digital technology does not permit.

These physical items and constructed environments may be drawn from our surrounding world, but this is not always the case. In some instances, material culture is made available to us from times, places, and people quite removed from our familiar era and landscape. In such cases, the actual object or space may have been formed decades, centuries, or millennia ago, yet it survives as an authentic connection with us today by way of its presence in our contemporary world. In similar fashion, an object or space may function as a physical record of actions that occurred in distant locations around the globe, serving to extend our notions regarding the immense, sometimes similar, and at other times diverse range of individuals on the planet. Consider, for example, new research that supports *Homo sapiens neanderthalensis* (Neanderthals) inhabiting organized communities and as crafters making and using tools. Previously, such implements were attributed to *Homo sapiens* (humans) because Neanderthals were thought to lack intelligence and to live in very primitive communities at best.

The actual objects and constructed spaces of various people may also become useful points of intersection between individuals and cultural groups, as these tangible productions of their lives serve as thoughtful and worthwhile locations for conversation, questioning, and productive dialogue. The delving across time, location, and culture that can readily occur through thoughtful investigations into tangible objects and spaces demonstrates the power and benefit that emerges from the study of material culture.

Key Idea 12: Exploring a Variety of Approaches to the Study of Material Culture

There are myriad ways that objects and spaces may be explored and analyzed. Included in Chapter 7 of this book are 10 diverse descriptions of how material culture could be investigated, which have been developed and utilized over time by individuals in various fields. These strategies are drawn from anthropology, museum studies, popular culture, American studies, folklore, history, environmental aesthetics, and art history. We include this broad number and diverse range of methods for analyzing objects and spaces to present the reader with possibilities for investigating the surrounding world in thoughtful and meaningful ways. Some of these approaches will be more or less applicable in their use with specific objects and spaces; others are broader in their potential application. Readers of this book are encouraged to utilize the various strategies discussed here with objects and spaces, to determine which approaches seem most compatible and beneficial for exploring particular objects and spaces in ways that generate the greatest meaning for themselves and their students.

CONCLUSION

The investigation of material culture within art education provides the impetus and opportunity to throw wide open the door of questioning, and in so doing expand the vast possibilities of asking and exploring what art education might become. It challenges, in meaningful ways, taken-for-granted and long-entrenched ideas that have given shape to art education for many years. Some art educators may embrace such change; others will likely be threatened by it. But thoughtfully considered questioning of our field provides the possibility for increased discussion and reassessment of what we purposefully choose to teach and, consequently, what we knowingly omit from art instruction. An emerging conversation about the role of material culture in art education, held in concert with others and with our reflective selves, helps provoke a much-needed reappraisal of our field, ourselves, and what we teach our students. It is our desire that what is included in the pages that follow will serve as an impetus and catalyst for generating meaningful instructional practice and continued conversation about the exploration and study of material culture within art education and, more important, within the lives of learners.

CHAPTER 2

Objects and the Stories of Our Lives

Two fundamental features help define all individuals and their place in the world. These deep personal characteristics of humanity are revealed through examining the objects we possess and life stories we tell that together help construct the essence of our individual and collective worlds. The objects each of us keeps in view or hidden from sight speak in some degree to the values, interests, convictions, and customs we embrace. Our choices to own, display, conceal, or discard the various things in our lives is based, in large part, on what we value and believe. What do the things I possess, and the decisions I make concerning them, reveal about me and what I value? How are my attitudes, beliefs, and actions displayed through the things I keep around me? In what ways are the things I possess similar to or different from those of my friends and acquaintances? Consider what is kept and displayed in my residence, office, automobile, or even what is tucked away in my closet, attic, or basement. What I determine to keep and reveal to others (or not show to them), as well as how I decide to display these objects, is a reflection of what I prize and hold dear.

Conversely, the discarding of objects also causes each of us to pause and reflect on the values we maintain in making a decision to jettison these things. Why do I keep some objects in my possession and discard others? On what basis do I make such decisions? Why are certain things kept as special for a particular amount of time, and then let go at some point in life? Even our manner of disposing of an object—whether it is recycled, deposited in the trash, given away (to whom?), or sold—reveals something about how we view the world and account for our actions within it.

The abundance of objects in our lives helps define who we have been, who we are now, and perhaps who we desire to be someday. No matter our age, gender, or wealth, whether we are introverted or extroverted, of high intellectual standing or not, socially well connected or living in isolation, we often conduct our identity-building and view ourselves through the lens of the resonant value and vibrant meaning of the objects—whether many or few—we maintain around us.

The worth of an object may be determined by its monetary appraisal. This is not always the case, however. There are times when an object's value is determined more by its personal significance to the individual or group possessing it, rather than by its financial worth. An inexpensive souvenir brought back from a family trip and placed visibly in the house to remind the group of their travel experience together, the small colorful stone given to a parent by a young child while they wait together at the bus stop, the "lucky" penny found on the street by a woman on her 21st birthday and kept for many years as a conscious memento of that day do not in and of themselves hold much monetary value. In fact, they may possess zero worth as far as a dollar-and-cents appraisal. Instead, they are made valuable in another way, and this is where story comes to play a significant role in our lives.

It is often the stories that surround an object that greatly affect how this item is viewed and regarded. For instance, an old guitar resting in the corner of the room may seem of little value until the story is told that this particular instrument was played by Jimi Hendrix during a concert in London in 1967. A fountain pen on the shelf may look like any number of such ubiquitous writing implements until it is learned through storytelling that this particular pen was used by President Kennedy to record his autograph during a chance meeting with a woman on the street in Washington, DC, in 1962, and that she has proudly kept both pen and presidential autograph since then. The Girl Scout beret situated in an old wooden box does not capture much attention until the story is revealed that the hat once belonged to Juliette Gordon Low, founder of the Girl Scouts. The objects we possess, and that sometimes drive the actions of our lives, often appreciate in perceived significance through the stories that reverberate around them.

The same can be said of objects in our lives whose stories are not tied to well-known musicians, revered politicians, or people of historical renown. Such objects and their related stories may be drawn from our personal memory and everyday experiences of life. The sight and touch of a well-worn pair of jeans or a certain sweatshirt may call back memories of specific life incidents that occurred while wearing them. The smell of fresh-cut evergreen sprigs can, for some, evoke stories of wintertime holiday events in years gone by. A song heard today, but listened to on the radio as a teenager decades ago, has the ability to bring to mind a flood of stories from that earlier era in life. The material culture of our lives, coupled often with related stories, can be powerful in shaping how we view the world and perceive our place within it.

Because objects are of such import in our lives, it is necessary that we not overlook the potential value that comes through a deep and conscious investigation of them. This is true even if the particular object seems inconsequential or is assigned little value in our experience today, because it may be in these easily overlooked objects that we find significance later in life. James Deetz (1977) speaks to this matter quite eloquently:

It is terribly important that the "small things forgotten" be remembered. For in the seemingly little and insignificant things that accumulate to create a lifetime, the essence of our existence is captured. We must remember these bits and pieces, and we must use them in new and imaginative ways so that a different appreciation for what life is today, and was in the past, can be achieved. (p. 161)

Our task, then, is to explore in earnest the objects we possess around us and the significance of these things in our lives. By examining the stories that surround these objects, we can determine the richness of their meaning and the broad extent of their worth.

APPROACHING OBJECTS

We (the authors) often ask our students to explore objects. Through such experiences, individuals investigate the personal meanings and significance drawn from various self-selected objects within their own lives, often sharing with others the stories of what they have researched and discovered. These object investigations have provided us and our students with some powerful and rewarding educational encounters. Although there are numerous ways to explore objects and related stories, we share six of them here that we have used in our teaching. Readers are encouraged to utilize one or more of these approaches to object investigation with students, and consider possibilities for how these various approaches could be combined, altered, and added to in ways that best match the needs, interests, and age levels of your students.

Approach 1: Investigating a Single Object of Personal Significance

In this learning activity, students are asked to select a specific object that holds personal significance for them. It might be an object from their home or bedroom, one given to them by a family member or close friend, something received as an award, or perhaps an object that the student has made. This chosen object might have particular significance for others as well, but students are instructed to focus on selecting an object that is of importance to them personally. The more intrinsically valuable the object is to the student, the more meaningful this learning activity can be for the student and for those with whom they share their stories. Once the object for study is selected, the student is directed to write a short paper about this object in rich, personal terms. Students are encouraged to be very descriptive in their discussion of the object: Why is this object significant to you? What is the particular story behind its significance? When and how did you come to possess this object? How did acquiring this object make you feel then, and now? Is it an object that has become more or less meaningful to you over time? Why is this so? To assist students in writing this paper, we recommend that they read one or more chapters from Sherry Turkle's 2007 book *Evocative Objects*. Students are also instructed to include with their paper, if possible, a photograph, drawing, or painting of this object. When the assignment is due, students will briefly share their written response and their object (or their visual representation of the object) with the rest of the learning group, as well as hand in their papers.

Approach 2: Question-Driven Research of an Object

Research is most often initiated and directed through the questions we ask. It is the captivating search for answers that drives us to explore the world and all things in it. We apply this principle of question-driven research to object study here. In this learning activity, students are asked to identify a specific object they would like to know more about, particularly one whose purpose or function is unfamiliar to them. This approach to object exploration is most productive if the student has direct and immediate access to the actual object being investigated.

The first task of the student is to examine the object carefully and generate a list of questions (we usually use 20 questions as a starting place) that emerge from mindful consideration of the object and sensory contact with it. We recommend that students touch and/or handle the object, if possible. Encourage students to use a magnifying glass to view the object, if doing so may reveal more visually obscured information about the item. As part of the analytic process, students are asked to draw or paint a representation of the object in question. Doing so will often assist the student in seeing features of the object that were overlooked at first glance. Students should list questions that come to mind as they engage with the object. If needed, prompt students to consider features such as the object's weight, materials, markings, potential purposes, alterations made over time, color, history, ownership, condition, and the like. Students may find this exercise more demanding than first anticipated, but we have found it to be an exploration that stretches students to consider an object more thoroughly than what is seen through an initial scan of it.

Once students have completed the task of generating the stipulated number of questions about the object, their next task is one of investigation. Students are asked to prioritize their questions, starting with those of most interest or import to them. Once the top few questions are identified, these become the motivators that initiate the student's investigation of the object. In this way, research is generated from and conducted through the student's direct questions, making it an investigation into their specific interests and what they would like to know about

Figure 2.1. Students encountering the work of artist Leslie Dill at the University of Oregon Jordan Schnitzer Museum of Art.

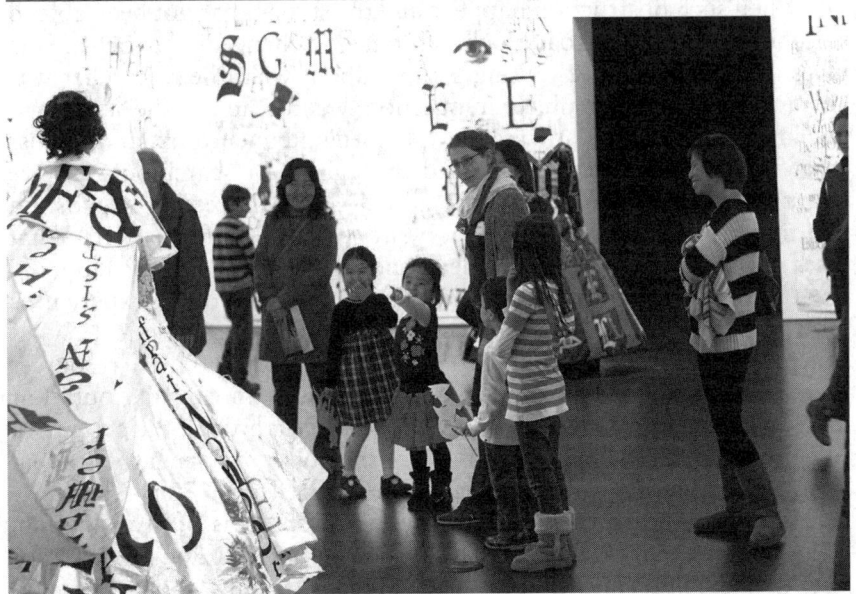

Photograph courtesy of the Jordan Schnitzer Museum of Art

the object. Throughout their exploration, students are encouraged to attach additional questions to their initial list. Fledgling investigators are often amazed at how the number of questions that surround the object increases significantly as they begin to learn more about it.

Approach 3: Learning the Value of the Search

Researchers sometimes learn firsthand that investigations into objects lead to dead-end disappointments. There are instances in the exploratory process when investigators are faced with time-delaying roadblocks, frustrating detours, and project-ending brick walls, rather than straight and unencumbered highways of inquiry leading to surprising and thrilling outcomes. As difficult as it may be to acknowledge and encounter these dead ends in the research path, such understanding is an important recognition for all researchers. The learning activity described here has emerged from instances when students have reached impassable obstacles in the research of a particular object. There have been times when a student has selected an object for study, done due diligence in questioning and exploring it, and yet reached an impasse in their investigation of the object. When such disappointing instances occur, we assure the student that she or he is not the first researcher to experience such frustration, and that a standstill in inquiry may sometimes be an outcome of research. Not all objects provide ready passage to their rich and, at times, hidden stories.

When such obstruction happens and the student has not been able to surmount the research roadblock, we suggest a change in the focus of the investigation. Instead of writing a paper about what the researcher was able to learn about the object in question, we instead ask the student to document the research process they planned and undertook, and discuss what was accomplished and gained through this research activity. We ask students to respond to questions such as: What research roads did you traverse? Where did you go in your search for information? What clues did you pursue and what dead ends did you encounter? How did you try to surmount the roadblock? What successes did you experience? How did the roadblocks and successes in research make you feel? What sources of information did you go to for assistance? Did these resources then lead you elsewhere? Who did you talk with in carrying out your investigation? In this way, the story that emerges through the activity of research is not so much directed toward the object and what the student uncovered about it; rather, it becomes a self-reflective story about the researcher and what was learned through the process of investigation. This *dead-end reflecting activity* has produced a rewarding outcome for our students, just as (if not more) revealing as learning about the initial object of their investigation.

Approach 4: Repurposing an Object

Objects are sometimes used in ways different from what was intended. Bathtubs become containers for holding outdoor plants and flowers; the set of metal prongs from a hand-held rake are removed from the handle, attached to the wall, and now used to hold sets of keys; colored glass bottles and jars, with a little adjustment, become decorative light fixtures. Our world is filled with objects utilized in ways not originally planned. E. McClung Fleming (1982) makes a distinction between objects employed as initially purposed and those whose current use does not match the intent for which they were designed. Considering this difference, the first type of object function Fleming designates as "uses (intended functions)," while the second form of function he terms "roles (unintended functions)" (p. 166), thus differentiating between an object's *use* that is satisfying its intended function and an object that is fulfilling a *role* when it is repurposed in a manner outside the initial intent. In this exploratory activity, students are called upon to both write and respond visually, considering Fleming's differentiation between an object's "use" and its altered "role."

The first part of the students' activity is directed toward recording an object's *use*. Students are each asked to select a well-recognized object in the world today, such as a bicycle, sewing machine, umbrella, or hair dryer, and produce a written description of it, discussing its design features, history, place in society, where it is often found, and so forth—what Fleming would refer to as its "use." Along with this written description of the object's use, students are asked to make a visual representation of the object through a drawing or painting of it.

The second feature of the assignment focuses on Fleming's (1982) notion of an object's "role." Students are asked to repurpose their selected object in some way—in other words, to change the object's form and role in the world. How is the object's purpose altered by these changes? Are features added to it or deleted from it? Is the object now placed in a new location or context? How has this altered location shifted the way the object is seen and utilized? What is the purpose for this change in the design of the object? Students are called on to respond through written description as well as visual depiction of this altered object. In this way, students are able both to show and tell about an object's shift from having a specifically designed *use*, to fulfilling a newly designated repurposed *role*.

Approach 5: Object as Storyteller

The investigation of objects and stories can take a somewhat imaginary twist as well. An approach by George Geahigan (1999) uses a work of art as the starting point for an exercise of imaginative self-reflection. By discussing an artwork in the first person, the work of art, or someone or something represented in the artwork, describes the scene or setting from the standpoint of what it would be like to be situated in the object or be part of it, rather than characterizing it as an external observer. In this way, the artwork offers a firsthand description and story of the thing itself, often utilizing the five senses as a way to "make extrapolations from what is literally represented in a work and to go beyond the cursory and shallow observations so typical of student responses" (p. 14). The outcomes of this activity can be quite provocative.

The same approach can be employed with other objects of material culture. In this learning activity, rather than having the student research the selected object and construct the story about it from the outside position of the researcher, the student assumes the perspective of the object, so that the object is, in effect, telling the story about itself. What is it like to be this object? When, where, and how was the object made? What materials were used? Who was the maker and what was the object's initial purpose? Has it undergone any repurposing over time? What does the object think? What feelings does it express? What is the object's relationship with people around it? Through the invocation of all the senses—sight, touch, taste, smell, and hearing, plus considerations of time and space—the writer can produce an object-reflective written narrative that can range from being playfully whimsical to pensive and thought-provoking.

Approach 6: Objects and Stories

In this learning activity, students explore objects and their related stories in vibrant and personal ways. This is a storytelling experience that does not require a written component.

At least 2 weeks prior to conducting this activity (more than 2 weeks is generally better, however), students are given the following instructions:

> On the day of this activity, bring three objects with you to class in response to any three of the following 15 statements (one object per statement). Think carefully about your selections and be prepared to show, discuss, and answer questions regarding these three objects you bring with you. Students are requested to not discuss or show their three objects to any other class members prior to the activity.
>
> Bring:
> 1. An object that belongs to you that you received as a gift.
> 2. An object that belongs to you that you carry with you all or most of the time.
> 3. An object that belongs to you that has religious or spiritual significance.
> 4. An object that belongs to you that at one time belonged to another family member.
> 5. An object that belongs to you that you received as an award.
> 6. An object that belongs to you that you made.
> 7. An object that belongs to you that you really should get rid of, but for some reason you cannot do so.
> 8. An object that belongs to you that you purchased used.
> 9. An object that belongs to you that you traded something else (other than money) to possess.
> 10. An object that belongs to you that is ugly.
> 11. An object that belongs to you that is very old.
> 12. An object that belongs to you that has special significance from your childhood.
> 13. An object that belongs to you that is part of a larger group of similar objects you collect.
> 14. An object that belongs to you that you think you will always keep.
> 15. An object that belongs to you that you carry for good luck.

This object-based storytelling activity is best conducted with class members seated in a circle, so that objects and stories can be easily shared. When participants arrive, each with his or her three objects, they are asked to join the circle. When all students are seated, the instructor gives the instructions. Here, the approach to story-sharing is based on a belief that stories told within the group are not independent and isolated narratives, but rather relate to one another and connect us in our affairs of life. Keeping this in mind, the key to this activity is the way the students' storytelling progresses and builds. Rather than beginning with one student and proceeding around the circle, the order in which students take their turn is determined by connections they make to one another's stories. Doing so displays a foundational twofold premise that undergirds this activity: (1) Objects and stories are related and supportive of one another in the forming of meaning. For this reason, objects are often made more meaningful by the stories that surround them. Conversely, stories frequently increase in significance when told in relation to the objects that give tangible substance to these stories. And (2): It is the stories that we tell to one another that help weave and fasten us collectively as people. The life stories we share often connect and resonate with listeners; in this way, it is the telling and grasping of these stories that helps link the lives and memories of individuals together.

To achieve the desired activity outcomes, one student in the circle acts as the starter. That person is asked to show their three objects, one at time, and tell the corresponding story about each of these objects. If possible, students are encouraged to pass their objects around the circle while telling the story, enabling everyone to examine the objects up close. Students are given the choice not to circulate their objects, however, if an item is fragile or the student declines to do so. The length of time per story is determined by the instructor, based on the number of students in the class and the overall time available for this activity. It is important to watch the clock carefully during this activity so that everyone in the group receives their allotted amount of time to show their three objects and tell their stories.

During a student's turn, the rest of the class is instructed to pay close attention to the stories that are told. Students are asked to listen carefully for some particular feature of the storyteller's narrative that connects to and resonates with something in a story he or she is prepared to tell about one of the three objects. This connection between one person's objects and stories and those of another student might occur through a particular type of object (for example, piece of jewelry, a toy, or sports trophy), a family member who previously owned the object (such as a grandparent, parent, sibling), or perhaps whether the object is considered old, ugly, of spiritual significance, or carried for good luck. For students to *listen carefully* to the stories that are told by their classmates and to *identify* connections between these narratives and their own stories is a primary objective of this activity. The instructor explains that if a student recognizes an intersection between a story being told and their own story, then this is the signal that they should proceed next, after the current student's turn has been completed. In this way, the narrative between students is connected, continuous, and fluid as the storytelling of the class unfolds. It becomes the opportunity to bridge across the narratives and braid together all the multilayered stories surrounding these objects as the various students' stories and objects are revealed, one after the other.

There may be times in this activity when connections between students' stories are not obvious or easily recognized. It is in such situations that students need to search for more obscure associations between their stories and those of their peers. This is where thoughtful analysis and the creative generation of connective ideas occur. It is the location where educators encourage students to stretch their reflective insights and take interpretive risks; it becomes a time when "aha moments" abound!

Considering the connected nature of the objects and stories that emerge within a class setting, we propose an additional artmaking activity using these objects. There have been times when we used the objects students brought to class as sources for drawing and painting experiences. In such cases, we positioned all the objects together in a collective still-life setup, for students to observe and draw or paint following the storytelling experience. When doing so, students are encouraged not only to consider the visual relationship of the various objects as they reside together in the still-life composition, but also to remember and contemplate the connectedness of the stories they have just heard surrounding these objects as they relate to each other.

This object and storytelling activity is, in the many times we have conducted it, one of the most engaging, rewarding, and revealing learning experiences we have ever experienced. Through it, students have come to know a great deal more about one another and at times gained deeper self-understanding. The life-formed stories we each possess, as well as the life-related stories told to us by others that resonate with our own life stories, fuse together in meaningful and often declarative ways. Our memories, values, activities, and longings—the core of our humanity—are displayed through the things we possess and the stories we choose to tell about them. In distilling the outcomes of this object and storytelling experience over the years, we have developed the following "Five Fundamental Beliefs about the Intertwined Nature of People, Stories, and Objects." These guiding principles are potent reminders about the value of objects and stories to our lives:

1. Each of us is shaped by the objects we make, use, respond to, acquire, preserve, discard, and lose.
2. Our memory contains a myriad of life-formed and life-related stories, which also help shape who we are and who we will become.
3. Many of these life stories are associated directly and inseparably with objects.
4. Many of these objects that are meaningful to us are made meaningful by the significance of the stories that surround these objects.
5. Sensory contact with objects often triggers the memory of specific life stories, which, if told, then trigger in others the memory of their own life stories. In this way, stories become the fabric that weaves and entwines people together.

Through conversation, laughter, and at times tears brought on by our engagements with objects and their stories, we offer these five considerations to help students learn the significance of understanding the objects and stories of our lives.

CONCLUSION

Objects are powerful entities in each of our lives. The same can be said of our life-formed stories. When brought together, objects and stories have the strength and potential to shape us in dynamic and resolute ways. Encounters with objects—from both our past and present—may trigger strong responses that range from overwhelming euphoria and joy to oppressive and sometimes debilitating sorrow. Yet most objects of personal significance rest somewhere between these extremes in affecting how we conduct ourselves day-to-day. For this reason, the large majority of objects in our lives may be easily overlooked and brushed aside as unimportant. But the influence and value of these easily slighted objects in our daily experience should not be ignored and trivialized, for as Deetz (1977) reminded us earlier in this chapter, it is in the "seemingly little and insignificant things that accumulate to create a lifetime [that] the essence of our existence is captured" (p. 161). All things encountered in our world, and the entire breadth of stories that surround them, become valuable in considering ourselves and our place with others in the world. For this reason, we should each be constantly alert to identify and distill rich meaning from all our experiences with the objects and the stories that manifest themselves in our lives each day.

CHAPTER 3

Collecting and Collections

Considering material culture is enriched by a discussion of collectors and collecting. This was emphasized in Key Idea 6 (Respecting the Significance of Collecting and Collections) in Chapter 1. We expand on this key idea here by introducing objects from our own collections. In doing so, we are encouraging an appreciation of the objects (material culture) in our lives from a personal point of view. We progress from our own collections to theoretical views on collecting and examples of collecting or collections. Our goal is to demonstrate the importance of collections in signifying personal and communal values, attitudes, and beliefs; as sources of inspiration; connecting people with their heritage; and sources of memory, commemoration, comfort, and safety. There is a rich body of literature associated with collecting and collections. This chapter includes references and quotes chosen from this literature to exemplify discourse around the topic from a variety of perspectives.

We initiate our discussion with the ceramic palm-sized butterscotch-colored dog that sits on Doug Blandy's desk. This dog crouches, cocks its head slightly to the left, and stares into the distance. Made from a mold, this small canine with two mauled ears has a coat patinaed by being held and played with an impossible-to-know number of times. Inscribed on its underside are "WPA," "1937," and "N.D." This inscription indicates that its origins are in North Dakota in 1937 as a part of a Works Progress Administration (WPA) project. In 1937, North Dakota was experiencing the full force of the Great Depression.

Six years before the creation of the butterscotch dog, Laura Hughes Taylor, a student of pottery at Valley City Normal School, enrolled in the ceramics department at the University of North Dakota. After graduation, Taylor took a position with the Dickinson Clay Products Company. Her tenure was short, because in 1936 the WPA hired Taylor to supervise a ceramics project employing 11 women and one man at the Woodrow Wilson High School in Dickinson. The works produced at the high school were glazed and fired at Dickinson Clay Products. Six months later, the project moved to Mandan and was housed in the basement of the Central Grade School building. At that point, there were nine WPA workers, with that number eventually increasing to 12. As in the project's previous location, there was no kiln, so works were sent to the University of North Dakota for firing and glazing. In 1939, Taylor represented the WPA in a pottery demonstration at the New York World's Fair. The WPA ceramics project continued until 1942 (Olson & Olson, 2014).

The ceramics, including the butterscotch dog (Figure 3.1), produced under the auspices of the WPA in North Dakota, could not be sold. Instead, they were sent to libraries, nursery schools, and state hospitals. Animals like this butterscotch dog were sent to nursery schools, often as a part of larger sets of figurines for education and play (Olson & Olson, 2014). It is likely that, given Taylor's later work in designing similar-looking animals for Rosemeade Pottery, the butterscotch dog is of her own design.

For Doug, the importance of the butterscotch dog is that it signifies that community and government-based support for the arts and arts education can be effective. It is both a source of personal inspiration to him and a tool for teaching students interested in community arts about the heritage associated with such work. It also holds an important place in Doug's small collection of vintage objects associated with art education. This collection includes textbooks, rulers, and pencil boxes, among other items.

Paul Bolin also collects. As a child, he began a collection of coins from the United States and Canada, many of which he still possesses today. He tells the story of his mother noticing his predilection for picking up things and placing them in his pockets on the way home from school. To this day, he carries in his pockets specific objects that have personal meaning.

Figure 3.1. Butterscotch dog.

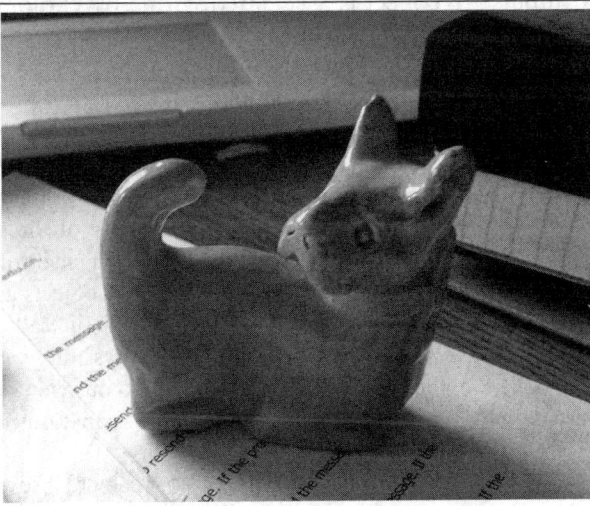

Photograph courtesy of Doug Blandy

What follows only begins to suggest the relevance of subjectivity in approaching the appreciation and understanding of material culture as it manifests in the impulse to collect. In this regard, Jean Baudrillard (1994) observes:

> The objects in our lives, as distinct from the way we make use of them at a given moment, represent something much more, something profoundly related to subjectivity: for while the object is a resistant material body, it is also, simultaneously, a mental realm over which I hold sway, a thing whose meaning is governed by myself alone. It is all my own, the object of my passion. (p. 7)

OBJECTS OF PASSION

The gathering of objects extracted from their original context and recontextualized in relationship to the collector's interests is ubiquitous across history and cultures. Collecting and collections are of interest to historians, psychologists, neurologists, and educators. For example, historian, James Clifford (1988) is confident that "[s]ome sort of "gathering" around the self and the group—the assemblage of a material "world," the marking-off of a subjective domain that is not "other"—is probably universal" (p. 218). Clifford helps us understand that collecting allows us to recognize that we are both like and unlike those around us, individually and communally.

Of course, integral to the act of collecting is the thing that is collected as well as the motivation to collect. Mihaly Csikszentmihalyi (1993) believes our impulse to collect is associated with a psychological dependence on objects. In his view, "Most of the things we make these days do not make life better in any material sense but instead serve to stabilize and order the mind" (p. 22). In this regard,

> Artifacts help objectify the self in at least three major ways. They do so first by demonstrating the owner's power, vital erotic energy, and place in the social hierarchy. Second, objects reveal the continuity of the self through time, by providing foci of involvement in the present, mementos and souvenirs of the past, and signposts to future goals. Third, objects give concrete evidence of one's place in a social network as symbols (literally, the joining together) of valued relationships. In these three ways things stabilize our sense of who we are; they give a permanent shape to our views of ourselves that otherwise would quickly dissolve in the flux of consciousness. (p. 23)

Are humans unique in their proclivity to collect? Steven W. Anderson, Hanna Damasio, and Antonio R. Damasio (2005) recognize collecting behavior in humans as well as in other species (for example, crows and ravens). They believe their research demonstrates that collecting is "supported by subcortical systems involved in biological regulation. In humans, however, it is apparent that the 'collecting drives' are modulated by cognitive processes that take social and other environmental factors into account and require the agency of other neural systems" (p. 202). Their research also assists us in understanding the difference between collecting and hoarding. Their research supports a hypothesis "that abnormal collecting behavior can result from damage to mesial prefrontal regions" of the brain (p. 207). In our experience, collectors are those who bring to their collections a sense of organization and satisfaction. The collections of hoarders, on the other hand, are less a source of satisfaction and more often illustrate an unsatisfied compulsiveness.

The ubiquitous experience of collecting also crosses age groups, with implications for education. About children and collecting, Clifford (1988) recognizes that

> Children's collections are revealing in this light: a boy's accumulation of miniature cars, a girl's dolls, a summer vacation "nature museum" (with labeled stones and shells, a hummingbird in a bottle), a treasured bowl filled with the bright shavings of crayons. In these small rituals we observe the channelings of obsession, an exercise in how to make the world one's own, to gather things around oneself tastefully, appropriately. (p. 218)

Collections can be important sources of knowledge and understanding within educational contexts. Michele and Robert Root-Bernstein (2011) provide additional insight into the importance of collecting to children and youth as well as the relationship between collecting and pedagogy. In their view, teachers can design an educational environment around the collecting interests of students. Through collecting, children learn to systematize and categorize things and ideas based on attributes such as color, emotions, letters, and sounds. Collected objects can also be the source of games and be used as storytelling devices. Root-Bernstein and Root-Bernstein advocate for an approach that promotes "free-choice" collecting. They see free-choice collecting as a "kind of play that results in something to play with." Such play leads to the "intrinsic satisfaction of the thing itself" inspiring "an absorbing make believe" that "exercises critical and cognitive skills" (p. 1).

Jeanne Nemeth (2011), writing within the context of art education, encourages art educators to acknowledge collecting behavior in children as a way to assist children and youth in understanding and appreciating their histories and communal experiences while simultaneously providing a link to aesthetics and art.

The relationship of collecting to art is well known. Historically, art collections have been associated with royalty, merchants, scholars, museums, educational institutions, government entities, as well as corporations. Private collections tend to be ephemeral and are eventually dispersed through the market or become the core or important amendments to public collections. For example, the Frick Collection and the Morgan Library in New York City, and the Phillips Collection and Freer Gallery of Art in Washington, DC, all began as private collections. Andrew W. Mellon's collection of European paintings and sculpture is core to the National Gallery of Art in Washington, DC. Robert Lehman's collection of paintings, textiles, sculpture, and decorative arts is integral to the Metropolitan Museum of Art in New York City.

A relatively recent example of a private collection moving into the public domain is the case of the Herbert and Dorothy Vogel collection. Herbert Vogel made his living as a postal worker and Dorothy Vogel as a librarian. Over a 45-year period, despite a relatively modest income, they amassed a collection of 4,000 pieces of contemporary art that have now been donated to museums across the United States, including the National Gallery of Art, the Museum of Contemporary Art in Los Angeles, the New Orleans Museum of Art, and the Harvard Art Museum (Vogel, 2008).

Some museum collections of art are distinguished by the encyclopedic nature of their holdings, such as those found at the Metropolitan Museum of Art, while others are more specialized based on time period (for example, the Museum of Modern Art), geographic location (such as the Sackler Gallery, Washington, DC, with its focus on Asia), or category (for example, the American Folk Art Museum).

BEYOND THE VISUAL IN MATERIAL CULTURE STUDIES

Given the primacy of the visual, it is not surprising that when one thinks of collections, what most frequently comes to mind are collections associated with the visual. However, recognizing that culture is fomented and expressed beyond the visual is distinctive of material culture. The *Cabinets of curiosities* or *Wunderkammers*, originating during the European Renaissance, exemplify collections of multisensory detritus that included geologic specimens, artworks, religious icons, perfumes, antiques, biological specimens, zoological specimens, clocks, automata, architectural miniatures, ethnographic artifacts, and medical specimens, among most anything else that can be imagined.

Associated with these cabinets were gatherings where the curiosities were removed from their cases and experienced firsthand by guests of the owner. This tradition has continued to the present day through the installations of artist Mark Dion in various museums, including the Weisman in Minneapolis and the Wexner Center in Columbus, as well as David Hildegrand Wilson's Museum of Jurassic Technology in Los Angeles.

Given the multisensory character of material culture in that it extends beyond the visual, collections may focus on one of the other bodily senses. Consider, for example, the sense of smell, possibly the most devalued of the human senses. The *Stasi*, or East German secret police, maintained a collection of the smells of selected Germans in case they were ever needed for tracking by hunting dogs (Doctorow, 2007). Artist Andy Warhol (1975) wrote about creating a smell collection. Artist Sissel Tolaas, known as the world's preeminent odor artist, has amassed a collection of more than 7,000 scents that include human perspiration, dirt, toys, and rotten bananas (McGrane, 2007). Current projects include collecting smells from cities throughout the world such as Cape Town, Istanbul, Nuuk, Mexico City, and Detroit (Gera, 2013).

Smell and the City (smellandthecity.wordpress.com/) is a web-based project dedicated to building enthusiasm for smell. Participants on the website post advice on collecting smells, smell narratives, and smell pedagogy.

COLLECTORS AND COLLECTING ON THE INTERNET

Smell and the City exemplifies how the Internet has been a boon to collectors and collecting. Consider, for example, the commercial craft-oriented website Etsy. A search on Etsy for "collectibles" returns close to three-quarters of a million references across eight specific categories such as "art," "accessories," and "ceramics and pottery," as well as more comprehensive categories like "everything else," "collectibles," and "handmade." Although Marjorie Akin (1996) may ultimately be correct in arguing, at least for manufactured collectibles, that "There is no way to gauge the percentage of humanly manufactured goods that have passed through collections at some point," she concedes that "the volume must be staggering" (p. 102). Indeed, a Google search for "collections" or "collectibles" suggests the myriad objects that are collected as well as the breadth and depth of the collecting impulse like never before. Similar searches on Pinterest, Instagram, YouTube, Flickr, and Facebook reveal, using Akin's word, "staggering" results.

Collectors are also using the Internet as a way to display collections. TYPOLOGY consists of the website thetypology.com along with a constellation of social media. The topologist is Diana Zlatanovski, a self-described musicologist, anthropologist, and photographer. According to her website, she is also a curatorial research associate at the Museum of Fine Arts in Boston. Zlatanovski (n.d.) describes *typology* as a photographic collection of collections. Working with cultural artifacts as a researcher and museum curator, I've developed a tremendous appreciation for the significance of objects.... By definition, a typology is an assemblage based on a shared attribute. Patterns, both visual and intellectual, resonate and reveal themselves within collections. Information not apparent in isolation becomes visible in context—only through studying groupings are we able to discern similarities and contrasts. In observing collections of similar things, the beautiful variations become evident. And the closer you look, the more you see.

Visitors to TYPOLOGY encounter groupings of like objects arrayed in rows on a white background. Underneath each array is a short comment having to do with the objects. For example, nine wrenches (www.thetypology.com/WRENCH) of different sizes and shapes are organized in one horizontal row accompanied by text that describes what inspired Zlatanovski's display, a comment on early tools, and information on when wrenches were first patented and by whom (Solymon Merrick in 1835). Zlatanovski (n.d.) passes judgment on the collection as "A study in human ingenuity and evolution" (p. 1).

In another example, 12 blue mussel shells are three to a row in four rows (www.thetypology.com/BLUE-MUSSEL-SHELL). Through the accompanying text, visitors to the site learn that the coloring of the mussels is a result of their diet and erosion, and that mussels may live for 40 years. On another page, two rows of four Fisher body models are accompanied by a brief history of the Fisher Body Company (www.thetypology.com/FISHER-BODY-AUTO-MODELS). The founders of the company also created a foundation supporting craftsmanship and creativity. Until 1968, a dream car model contest for boys 12 to 19 was held. According to Zlatanovski, some contest winners went on to employment in the auto industry. On the TYPOLOGIST blog (thetypologist.tumblr.com/), collections displayed include 8 amulets (July 25, 2014), 12 photographs of bus stops (July 24, 2014), and 84 tent stakes, "A perfect segway for my return to reality after spending 2 weeks in Big Sur and Yosemite" (July 23, 2014). On Twitter, The Typologist (@TheTypology) tweeted on July 25, 2014:

> He #collected_his first skull in his 20s-dragging a harbor seal's head back to his parents' house on public transit ow.ly/zB3mw

and

> A beautiful Nubian jewelry exhibit is up at @mfaboston_I'm loving the amulet typology: tmblr.co/Z2vTcw1MTQoCr

Collecting and Collections 45

On Pinterest, Zlatanovski publishes Material Culture Typology (www.pinterest.com/thetypologist/material-culture-typology/). Here, visitors will find pins of soccer balls, antique German doll parts, pennies, thimbles, socks, shoes, clown eggs, and license plates, among other objects.

Another Internet-based collector is John Foster. Foster publishes regularly with the Design Observer Group (designobserver.com/). On his Design Observer Group page (designobserver.com/profile/johnfoster/275), he describes himself as a collector of self-taught art and vernacular photography. As a member of the Design Observer Group he publishes *ACCIDENTAL MYSTERIES* (www.accidentalmysteries.com/collections/).

Followers of Foster's find collections of images associated with sideshow banners, snapshots of clowns, handmade flash cards, science tattoos, domestic architecture decorative elements, and altered photographs.

COLLECTING IN THE MIDST OF CATASTROPHE AND GRIEF

Arguably the most challenging example to date of institutional collecting in the 21st century is associated with the attack on, and subsequent collapse of, the World Trade Center in New York City on September 11, 2001. As a case study, the efforts of regionally based institutions to collect the material culture associated with the events of that day in lower Manhattan epitomize both the private and public collecting response to such a catastrophic event. Creating a communal narrative while also honoring the individual thoughts and feelings associated with the days and weeks that followed was a primary motivation.

Over a decade after the attack, the National September 11 Memorial Museum opened to the public on May 21, 2014. Located on the site of the World Trade Center in New York City, the mission of the museum is, in part:

> to bear solemn witness to the terrorist attacks of September 11, 2001 and February 26, 1993. The Museum honors the nearly 3,000 victims of these attacks and all those who risked their lives to save others. It further recognizes the thousands who survived and all who demonstrated extraordinary compassion in the aftermath. . . . the Museum attests to the triumph of human dignity over human depravity and affirms an unwavering commitment to the fundamental value of human life. (9/11 Memorial)

Designed by the architectural firms Davis Brody Bond and Snohetta, the museum is part of a larger complex that includes two pools of cascading waterfalls each surrounded by a low wall with the engraved names of those who died. Each fountain occupies one of the footprints of the World Trade Center Towers. The portion of the museum visible from the plaza surrounding the two fountains is described as a "pavilion that resembles a collapsed building" (Kimmelman, 2014). This pavilion provides entry to a massive underground space in which most of the museum exhibits are located.

Occupying this lower inner space are the exhibits dedicated to telling the stories of 9/11. Tom Hennes of Thinc Design, the lead exhibition designer, faced numerous challenges in representing the day and its aftermath. These challenges included the development of strategies for assisting visitors in encountering the materials on display; recognizing differing responses to the attack and its aftermath; encouraging empathy; and honoring the lived experience of those who were there. Eight hundred objects coupled with numerous multimedia presentations create the experience articulated by Hennes. Altogether, the museum's collections consist of 12,000 objects (Farrell, 2014).

Remarkably, the collection of objects began on the day of the attack. Jan Ramirez, now the chief curator at the National 9/11 Memorial Museum, recalls that while working at the New-York Historical Society on the day of the attacks, a paper dust mask was brought to her and became the first artifact collected from that day by her institution (Farrell, 2014). Simultaneously, New York's City Municipal Archive began a collection that would ultimately consist of 700 boxes of 9/11 materials that includes flowers left at the site, missing persons posters, and letters sent to recovery workers (Farrell, 2014). An assistant commissioner of the New York City Department of Records remembers thinking as the 9/11 artifacts were collected, "Very quickly you realize what you are actually doing. Each item is a person, a family, you couldn't think about that" (Farrell, 2014). Kenneth Jackson, president emeritus of the New-York Historical Society, acknowledges that collecting in the midst of an event such as 9/11 cannot be done rationally. He quickly recognized that it was important to start collecting immediately because of the ephemeral nature of much material associated with the event; there was the "need to collect then or you wouldn't get it" (Danitz & Fein, 2008).

Nothing was too insignificant to be collected. Walking through the exhibits at the National September 11 Memorial Museum, visitors encounter rescuers' helmets, shoes, a baseball, papers from corporate offices, identification cards, purses, wallets, phones, crushed file cabinets, vehicles, toys, religious items, service patches, children's drawings, photographs, and twisted pieces of the buildings, among many, many other objects on display. Also collected are television news reports, public dispatches, and personal narratives from people who were present in the

Twin Towers on 9/11, as well as family members and rescue workers. In addition to the collecting being done by professional collectors associated with public cultural institutions, recovery workers at Ground Zero organized materials at the site (Danitz & Fein, 2008).

Fresh Kills Landfill occupies 175 acres on Staten Island in New York City. In the months following 9/11, 1.8 million tons of debris from the World Trade Center site were brought to this location. The mission of those working at this site was to "retrieve anything that would have meaning for family members and history" (Danitz & Fein, 2008). As a consequence, more than 75,000 personal effects were recovered. Material was sifted "down to the size of a marble" (Danitz & Fein, 2008).

Like most museums, the National 9/11 Memorial Museum operates with a collections management policy. This policy asserts that the museum

> collects, preserves, documents, exhibits, interprets and makes available as a public learning resource the material evidence, primary testimony and expanding historical record of response to the terrorist events of February 26, 1993, and September 11, 2001, and their global repercussions. (9/11 Memorial Museum, 2011)

The collection "is envisioned to function as an extensive reservoir of historical facts, trustworthy content and cumulative insight that will deepen over time, with uses beyond physical exhibition" (9/11 Memorial Museum, 2011). Important to the collection is

> the incorporation of multi-layered perspectives and individual stories of victims, survivors, responders, area residents and witnesses, conveyed through exhibits and other narrative mechanisms grounded in primary sources and authentic artifacts . . . sources include, but not be limited to, salvaged remnants of the buildings, physical objects, oral histories, artwork, architectural elements, film, video and audio footage, photographs, posters, handbills, memorabilia, signage and personal effects. (9/11 Memorial Museum, 2011)

Jan Ramirez, chief curator of the National 9/11 Memorial Museum, was asked how she and her associates and an advisory committee, including family members, survivors, began using the materials collected from Ground Zero to create a visitor experience. Ramirez says they "started by starting," because to do otherwise would have resulted in missing important material associated with the event (Glassman, 2014). Decision-making was difficult. For example, "The archeological relics in Hangar 17 at JFK Airport, brought from the rubble, was our foundational collection. So we had to start by saying, 'All right, we've got 22 damaged rescue vehicles, which one do we choose?' Do you choose the one that is a horribly damaged vehicle but everybody lived from that truck? That's a great outcome but is that the most telling story you actually want as a first encounter" (Glassman, 2014).

Three days before the museum was dedicated, Ramirez remembers walking into the alcove dedicated to Flight 93. She remembers only choosing the materials associated with the downing of the airliner and the relationship of those materials to events on the plane. For example, the alcove includes a part of the heavily damaged kitchen where a flight attendant heated water as a weapon to subdue the hijackers, the watch of one of the passengers who confronted the hijackers, and a notebook found after the crash. For Ramirez these objects created an unexpected and profound sensory experience (Glassman, 2014).

CONCLUSION

This chapter only begins to suggest the range of material culture that has, is, and will be collected. Associated with acknowledging this breadth of things collected is a recognition of the passions and motivations that lead people to collect. In this chapter we reflected on collecting and collections to emphasize the multisensory character of material culture, thus expanding notions of collecting and collections. The evolving nature of the Internet will undoubtedly expand our consideration of what is meant by collecting and collections. Discussions of collecting in times of catastrophe and grief is regretfully part of what it means to be human. Collections and collecting are an important feature of humanity, worthy of recognition and study. The discussion provided here encourages contemplation and conversation directed toward significant topics associated with the focus of this chapter.

CHAPTER 4

Material Culture
Investigations Spanning Time, People, and Location

A primary feature of material culture studies is the emphasis such investigation places on experiences with actual objects. Whenever possible within the study of material culture, individuals are urged to encounter objects through direct sensory contact, reaching beyond the limits of sight-based observation alone. When we explore material culture, objects are sometimes handled, listened to, smelled, and perhaps even tasted. Through such multisensory experiences, learners are afforded more extensive entryways into the study and apprehension of things in the world around them. This immediate contact and handling of objects is not always possible, yet those who desire to explore objects are encouraged to search out specific items for scrutiny that provide access to multisensory engagement, and consider utilizing the widest number of investigative approaches and opportunities available to them.

The probing and analysis of material culture gives investigators the opportunity to inquire about objects situated across time, people's experience, and physical location. Such examination may occur through contact with things created centuries ago or longer, or items fashioned in our world today. The study of material culture may involve inquiry into the objects, actions, and perhaps customs of people unfamiliar to us, or it may generate reflective introspection into our own personal beliefs, ideas, and behaviors through the interrogation of things we each acquire and embrace. The same wide spectrum of deliberation can be applied when considering the location where objects were produced or currently reside, as material culture is ripe for investigations of human-made things created in or secured from far distant locations. Alternatively, material culture studies may activate a search into the meaning and significance of objects found in our own local or immediate environment.

The benefits drawn from object study are expansive, revealing potentially wide historical recognitions and increased cultural understandings. Investigations into the material culture of individuals and groups unknown to us furnish fresh opportunities to see and comprehend the tangible expressions of these unfamiliar people. This contact with the material culture of others affords an avenue of amplified awareness toward recognizing the cultural values and activities expressed by the makers, users, and preservers of these objects. The beliefs and actions of people are materialized within the tangible objects of their culture. Recognizing this helps us pause and scrutinize these objectified ideas and behaviors, and investigate and learn from them. Understandings drawn from these objects may provide an important step toward demystifying the "other" and enabling an increased appreciation of those regarded as unfamiliar and perhaps different from us. The study of objects and the people involved with their construction, use, and preservation supplies us with contemplative passageways to connect with others across time, culture, and location in ways that cannot always be accomplished through ideationally based conversation alone.

OBJECT INVESTIGATION

Two specific objects are discussed in this chapter. These objects are presented to help illustrate the benefit of object study and to exemplify how objects may be explored across time, people's experience, and physical location. These discussions are included here to serve as a spark and motivation for educators to engage learners in hands-on object-directed learning.

The first object is a personal family heirloom—a child's rocking chair—whose presence crosses over time and location. We examine this object as a bridge that straddles worlds in both the past and present. As such, this small antique chair serves as a material link between people of multiple eras and becomes a hub of attention for historical reflection.

The second object is an animated book of a traditional Chinese folktale about the killing of a wolf. The discussion exposes cultural and symbolic understanding that can occur by investigating an object situated within a people group and location that may be unfamiliar to those not from the region of its origin. The conversation surrounding this object is presented here to reveal the significant meaning that this item holds for the people who create, use, and preserve it. Reading and viewing this folktale, as well as appreciating its original cultural context, expands our understanding of the practices, beliefs, and traditions of people that may be unfamiliar to us. The study of material culture—in this case, an animated Chinese folktale—provides a grounded opportunity to consider (and perhaps reconsider) the often partisan and sometimes even bigoted notions that emerge when denoting the meaning and merit of unfamiliar things, ideas, and, more important, the people associated with them. It is an impetus and opportunity to reflect thoughtfully on the symbolic and sometimes obscure meanings placed upon the objects in others' lives as

Material Culture

well as our own. The object serves as a point of reflection, and becomes a potential facilitator of cultural awareness and understanding for those who desire to bridge the gap of perceived cultural mystery and misunderstanding between others and ourselves.

Example 1: An Object Investigation Spanning Time and Location

In 1987, I (Paul Bolin) visited the Museum of Fine Arts, Boston. There, I encountered one of the museum's most recognized paintings, John Singer Sargent's *Daughters of Edward Darley Boit* (1882) in Figure 4.1.

The large format painting depicts the four daughters of the lawyer turned painter Edward Darley Boit, who was a friend of Sargent. The girls—Mary Louisa, Florence, Julia, and Jane—are situated within various poses in the composition, with three of the four young females directing their gaze outward from it. The only sister not peering toward the viewer is Florence (the oldest of the girls, age 14 at the time of the

Figure 4.1. *The Daughters of Edward Darley Boit*, 1882, by John Singer Sargent, American, 1856–1925.

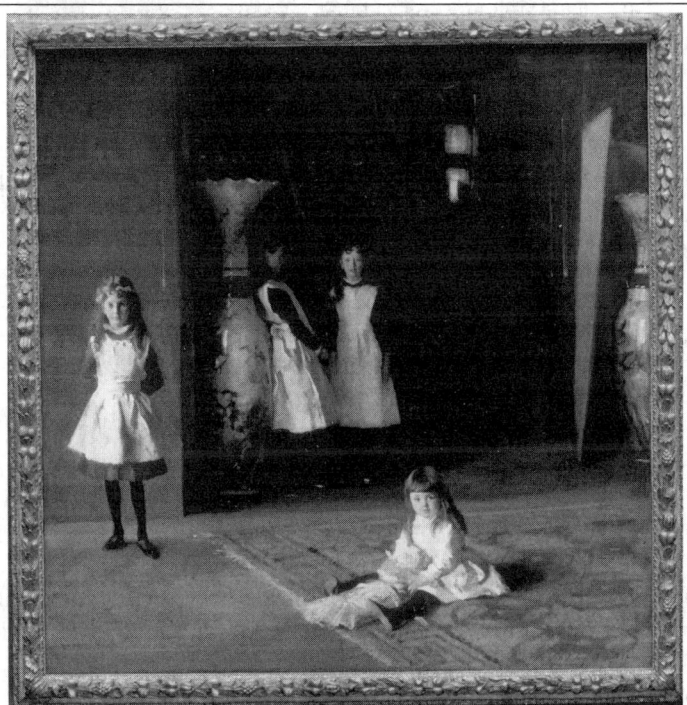

Oil on canvas, 221.93 x 222.57 cm (87 3/8 x 87 5/8 in.). Gift of Mary Louisa Boit, Julia Hubbard Boit, and Florence D. Boit in memory of their father, Edward Darley Boit. 19.124. Photograph © Museum of Fine Arts, Boston.

Figure 4.2. *Vases with decoration of birds and flowers*, Japanese, late Edo period to Meiji era, 19th century.

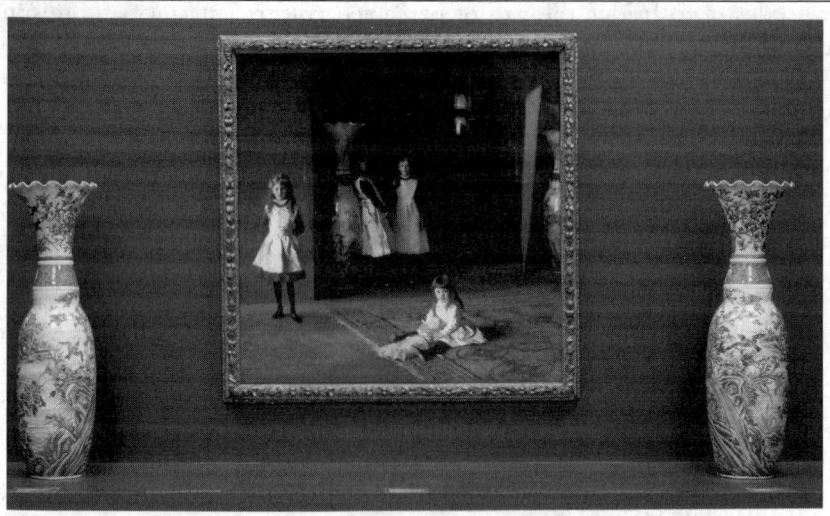

Arita ware, porcelain with underglaze blue decoration. 188 x 51 cm (74 x 20 1/16 in.). Gift of the Daughters of Julia O. Beals. 1997.212. Photograph © Museum of Fine Arts, Boston

painting), depicted leaning against one of two large blue and white Japanese vases that reside toward the background of the scene. Florence looks across the painting in the direction of the other towering vase at the far right of the canvas. The depiction of these two grandiose painted vases is striking, as their size and location dwarf the four girls and produce within the setting an aura of perplexing scale and unsettled composition.

The power and intrigue of the *Daughters of Edward Darley Boit* is intensified through another feature. As the painting is exhibited prominently at the Museum of Fine Arts, Boston, it is flanked on both sides by the actual Japanese vases depicted by Sargent in the work painted more than 130 years ago (Figure 4.2).

These impressive porcelain objects held a significant place in the Boit family throughout the late 19th and early 20th centuries and were gifted to the museum by the Boits in 1919. For me in the museum that day, and perhaps for many other visitors who encounter them, these two vases act as more than a novel framing device for the painting. These vases, as they are positioned alongside the work, serve as a vital link between the perceived past and the experienced present. I viewed them that day in 1987 as tangible physical objects that helped join two worlds, which, as a museum patron, I was attempting to straddle. One world was that of the past as it was painted by John Singer Sargent to include the vases in 1882, and the other a world of the present, where both I and the vases held place. Questions arose: In what ways do these two porcelain artifacts bordering the painting in the museum help span the distance between the worlds of the past and present? How do we view these two vases, as they exist in our contemporary world, because of their presence in this painting from a time more than a century ago? Is my relationship with this painting altered because of the immediate proximity in the museum of these two prominent objects depicted in the painting? Do I respond to this painting in some way that is different because of the presence of these objects both in my space and in that of the Boit girls? What relationships are perceived between tangible objects and visual reproductions of the same objects? These questions puzzled me at the time and have given me thoughtful pause since then.

Within a few months of my visit to the Museum of Fine Arts, Boston, my first child, Madeleine, was born. As a gift from one of my aunts, my wife and I received a small child's rocking chair (see Figure 4.3).

The tiny rocker had been in my family since the early 1900s; thus, when we received the chair, it had held a familial presence for more than 80 years. Attached to the underside of the chair is the following information:

Figure 4.3. Read family rocking chair (circa 1905).

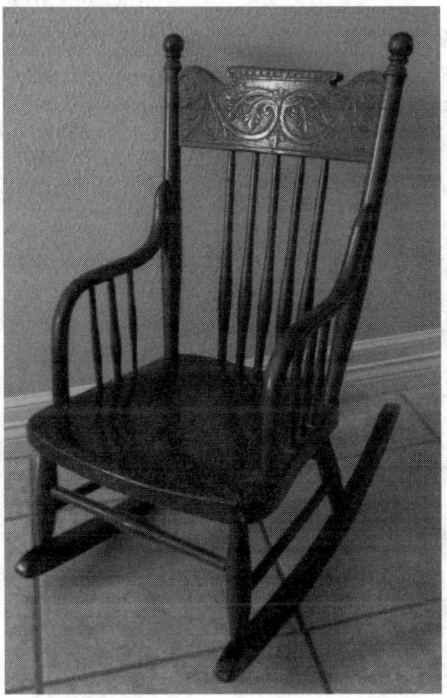

Photograph courtesy of Paul Bolin

This children's rocker was purchased by Hugh & Jenevieve Read for their 1st daughter, Luella J. (Keefe), born 11/20/05, probably in 1906 in York, Nebraska. This has been passed down to all the children, then to Luella's daughter, Kathryn Keefe Dey & then back to Ruth Read Johnsen. It is the desire of the family that this chair not be sold but will stay in the family & be passed on & enjoyed by any child who is a descendent of Hugh Read.

Hugh (1879–1950) and Jenevieve (1885–1964) Read are my grandparents (Figures 4.4 and 4.5). They were married on January 27, 1904, in rural southeast Nebraska, where they eked out a meager living on the family farm by performing various community jobs in the years prior to and during the Great Depression. Eight children were born to Hugh and Jenevieve between 1905 and 1924—three boys and five girls (including my mother). One daughter died as an infant. The torment of the Dust Bowl and its subsequent hardships sent Hugh, Jenevieve, and their youngest offspring on a migration to Oregon in 1940, where the family relocated to a small community outside Portland. Stories of early life for my grandparents, parents, aunts, and uncles were part of my growing up. Many families are like that.

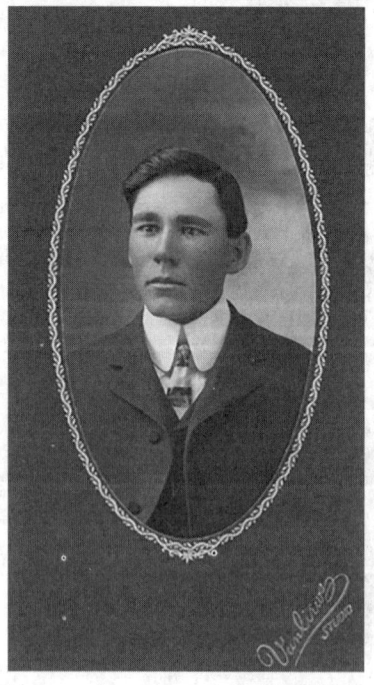

Figure 4.4. Hugh Read (1879–1950), circa 1900.

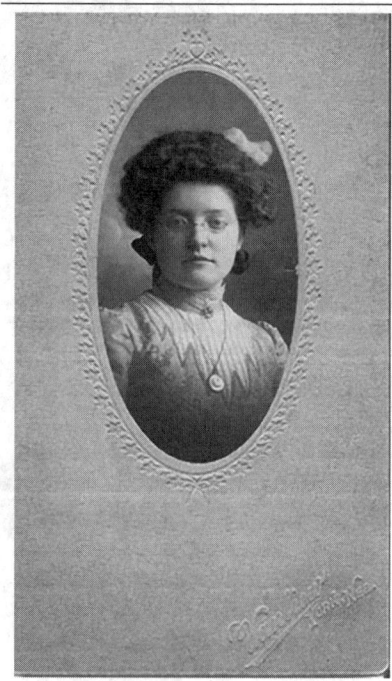

Figure 4.5. Jenevieve Read (1885–1964), circa 1900.

Photographs courtesy of Paul Bolin

Material Culture

The small rocking chair soon became a familiar fixture in the living room of our Oregon home, and the location for a picture of our young daughter Madeleine (Figure 4.6) in 1989.

A short time after the rocking chair's arrival to our house, a small box of old family photographs was included in a container of books and time-worn miscellaneous family items given to me by my aunt who passed the rocking chair to us. The little box held numerous black and white photo images of people who looked vaguely familiar: young portrayals of relatives I knew much later in life. The setting in many of these photographs was the stark and spacious landscape of rural Nebraska many years ago, made even more barren when pondered in black and white. I stared at these photos for affiliation, for association and connection with those I saw. But the world shown in these colorless photos was vastly removed from my life in Oregon. As much as I desired to connect with the people and places depicted in the photographs—many of them my relatives tracing back to the early 1900s—there was a prohibitive chasm that separated me from them. What I looked at was not my era, nor was it my location. Over the years, I had heard many family stories that traversed time and territory, bringing me some recognition of life in bygone days. I now held in my hands photographs of people, places, and activities that aided my understanding of the past, but these images were of a world and of things that still felt distant from me.

Figure 4.6. Madeleine Bolin (1989)

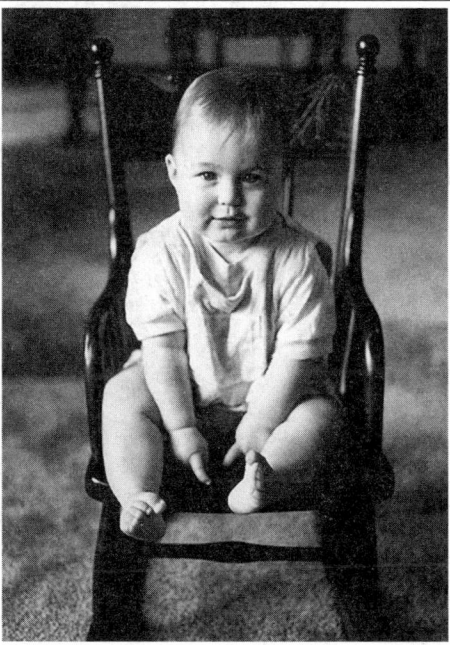

Photograph courtesy of Paul Bolin

Delving a few photographs deeper into the stack brought me an unexpected find. What appeared among the pile of images was a black and white photograph of my aunt Ruth at age 14 months, taken on the Read farm near York, Nebraska, in April 1913 (Figure 4.7). Situated along with my aunt in the outdoor scene is the little rocking chair, which at that time had been in the family for 7 years. Ruth is a younger sister of Luella, for whom the rocking chair was purchased in 1906.

Other photographs of the little rocking chair surfaced in the collection of images. I came upon the photo of an uncle, Max, (Figure 4.8) who is seated in the chair outdoors and next to the Read house in recognition of his seventh birthday on July 24, 1929 (Figure 4.8). Digging a little deeper in the box, I found a photograph of my cousin Kathryn, taken April 3, 1937 (Figure 4.9). She is bundled up on that spring day in Nebraska, celebrating her first birthday with the little rocking chair. Kathryn is Luella's daughter. To my knowledge, no photographs of the little rocking chair exist that were taken in the 52 years between 1937 and 1989.

I now had access to information about the rocking chair through images of it as well as the object itself. Conversations with my mother and aunt about the little chair revealed more family stories, particularly surrounding the Read children and the rocking chair. According

Figure 4.7. Ruth Read (April 1913)

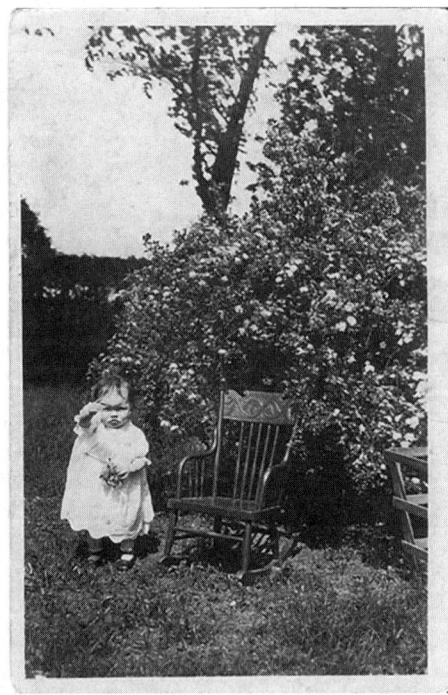

Photograph courtesy of Paul Bolin

Material Culture   57

to their reminiscences, for the financially burdened Read family living in rural Nebraska, the chair was a prized possession, especially for the children who had few store-bought items with which to play. The chair was circulated regularly among the seven Read children during their early years, with each sibling having primary possession of the chair for a prescribed length of time, usually 2 to 3 weeks, before it was circulated to the next child to enjoy. Birthdays with the chair (as seen in the photographs of Max and Kathryn) were memorable occasions, with the honoree receiving "ownership" of the chair for that special day.

Some alterations were made to the chair over time. It is difficult to determine for certain in these black and white photographs, but it appears the rocking chair was painted a light color in the time between 1929 and 1937 (see Figures 4.8 and 4.9). My mother remembers the chair being bright red at some point in her childhood. An aunt recalls that the rocking chair was once taken completely apart and reassembled by her brother Max. The little rocking chair and photographs of it helped my mother and aunt recollect and share with me memories about the past.

Figure 4.8. Max Read (July 24, 1929)

Figure 4.9. Kathryn Keefe (April 3, 1937)

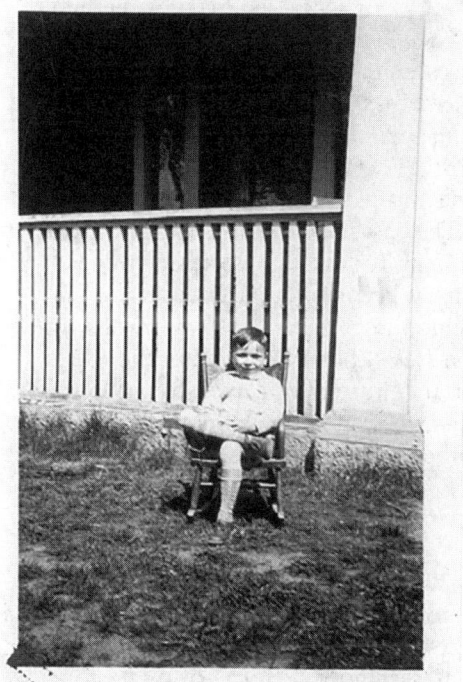

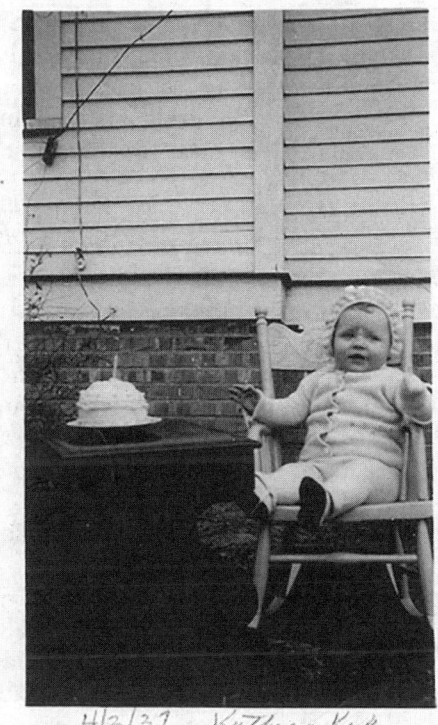

Photographs courtesy of Paul Bolin

The child's rocking chair and associated photographs did more than initiate the opportunity for my mother and aunt to recount to me personal remembrances of a time long ago. Narratives they shared and the photographs of family members with the little chair helped ally me with their past, but it was the presence of the chair itself that became a tangible connection to the early lives of my mother, aunts, uncles, and cousin. Stories about my ancestors were made vivid and substantive through a material object that linked me with them. Seeing photographs of the chair, my relatives, and their world growing up was helpful, but I experienced a much stronger link with the past through my contact with the actual chair. Here, I could hold in my hands the same object they had handled decades ago. I was able to touch the wooden contours of the chair and move my fingers over the hand-carved floral design, much like my relatives had done years ago (Figure 4.10). I could feel the various incised markings on the seat of the chair, indicating where members of my family had once sat and rocked in childhood contentment and birthday distinction throughout its decades of use. Physical access to the chair helped connect me to a time, location, and to family members from a distant era in a way that was not achieved through viewing photographs and hearing stories alone. Through sensory contact with an object from the past, a world from an earlier time became alive and real to me.

My experience with the little rocking chair reminded me of something else. The rocking chair's physical presence in my world connected me in a material way to lives lived long ago, as seen in the various photographs of my relatives in rural Nebraska. In reflection, I found this action strikingly similar to how the two blue and white Japanese porcelain vases, prominent in the Museum of Fine Arts, Boston, served to bridge my world as a museum visitor with the distant time and place depicted in John Singer Sargent's *Daughters of Edward Boit*. The vases and the little rocking chair both serve as physical connectors, helping to link the worlds of the past with those of the present. Through this, it becomes apparent that the material does matter. It is through tangible things—the physical objects we engage with through a variety of our senses—that we encounter the world in its resonant form. It is in the material culture of our lives, found in the past and present, close by or perhaps at a distance, wherein we grasp a rich and resonant understanding of others as well as ourselves.

Example 2: An Object Investigation Spanning People and Location

Educators committed to preparing students to be global citizens routinely contextualize material culture for the purpose of communicating about the lives of people associated with these expressions and important related traditions. Of particular interest, and the focus of this second example, are those instances in which collective and individual values from multiple cultural contexts collide.

Figure 4.10. Detail of Read family rocking chair

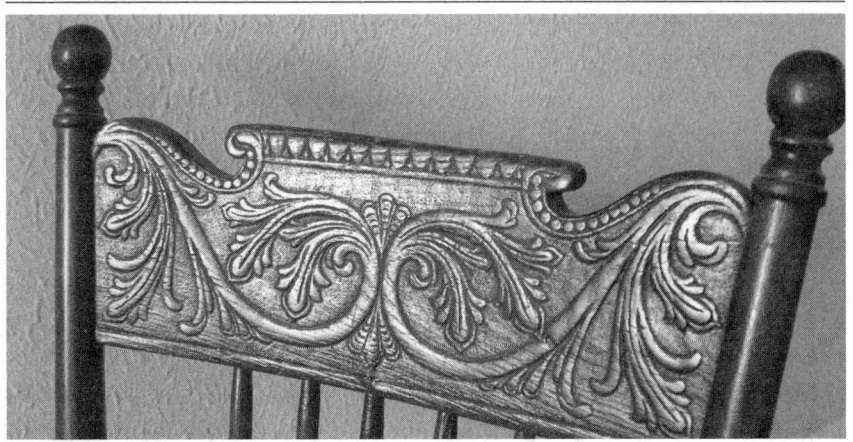

Photograph courtesy of Paul Bolin

Myths and folktales, inherently grounded in cultural values, are frequently a site of such collisions. Readers may be familiar with ongoing debates about the Walt Disney Corporation's appropriation of folktales and myths for commercial and entertainment purposes. Sometimes referred to as "Disneyfication," this process of interpretation often results in significant changes to stories from particular cultural groups or traditions in order to make the stories appealing for a mass audience. Consider, for example, the original tale of the three little pigs. In this tale, the houses of the first two pigs fall apart when a wolf blows on them. The two pigs are captured and eaten by the wolf. The wolf is then caught by the third pig after the wolf, attempting to enter the third pig's house from the roof, falls down the chimney. The wolf is then boiled to death in a cooking pot and eaten by the third pig. Compare this to the Disney adaptation of the tale in which the first two pigs escape to the third pig's house and the wolf only burns his rump and runs away.

It is not surprising that wolves, given a territorial range that includes North America, Europe, and Asia, figure prominently in myths and folktales across an abundance of cultures. In the People's Republic of China (PRC), isolated pockets of wolves exist throughout the country. A well-known story in China is the story of the Wolf of Zongshan—a tale with a lesson about the dangers of soft-heartedness in the presence of evil.

In this story, dating to at least the 15th century, a king encounters a wolf during a hunt. The king unsuccessfully attempts to kill the wolf with a bow and arrow, and the wolf escapes into the woods and encounters a scholar—Mr. Dongguo. The wolf, appealing to the scholar's love of all things, pleads for his life. The scholar hides the wolf in his book bag. Once the hunting party has passed, the wolf pleads for his life again—this time from starvation. Offered a pastry, the wolf says he only eats meat.

Alarmed, the scholar asks if he intends to eat the donkey. The wolf replies that donkey meat is not suitable and that he intends to eat Mr. Dongguo. A philosophical debate ensues and Mr. Dongguo and the wolf decide to present their case to three elders. The first elder, an apricot tree, sides with the wolf. The second elder, a water buffalo, also sides with the wolf. The last elder, a farmer, when told the story, is skeptical about the wolf being able to fit inside the book bag. To prove his point, the wolf jumps into the bag, upon which the farmer ties it shut and proceeds to beat the bag with a hoe. Eventually, the farmer pulls the seriously injured wolf out of the bag. Mr. Dongguo feels pity for the wolf until a woman overcome with grief tells him and the farmer how the wolf had dragged off her son. Mr. Dongguo, no longer feeling sorry for the wolf, picks up the hoe and finishes the wolf off with a blow to the head.

Another story about the wolf in China is associated with Lang Village in Guan County in Shandong Province. It is this story that exemplifies a collision between the story as it was told to me (Blandy) in China and an interpretation of that story for children and youth in the United States that was posted on a website about China's cultural heritage.

Lang, a word that translates as "wolf," is named after a folktale that can be found in the surrounding region and is well known among locals. During the Warring States Period of Chinese history, wolves were tormenting Lang Village and attacking and killing children. To save the children, the villagers made representations of children out of cooking dough, laced them with poison, and fed them to the wolves, thus killing the wolves. Another version of the story has dough characters created in the form of tigers to scare away the wolves.

Though the making of dough figures, or dough tigers, in Lang Village was once common, Liang Xiucai is one of the few remaining villagers continuing the tradition today (Figure 4.11).

He and his wife now sell the figures as toys at local markets. Liang Xiucai describes the figures that he makes as representing virtues important to Chinese culture and Lang Village history. Scholars at the Folk Art Research Institute at Shandong University of Art and Design estimate that Liang Xiucai has produced more than 2,000 different dough figure shapes.

I have conducted fieldwork in Lang Village as a part of a larger research project titled ChinaVine, an educational project dedicated to the documentation and interpretation of China's cultural heritage on the website ChinaVine.org. Kristin Congdon and I are the cofounders of this project.

On ChinaVine.org is an animated book called *The Wolf and the Dough Children* (chinavine.org/2011/06/16/wolf-and-dough-children/), as a part of the interpretation of Lang Village and the dough figures created by Liang Xiucai (chinavine.org/artist/dough-figures-liang-xiucai/).

Figure 4.11. Liang Xiucai painting a dough figure

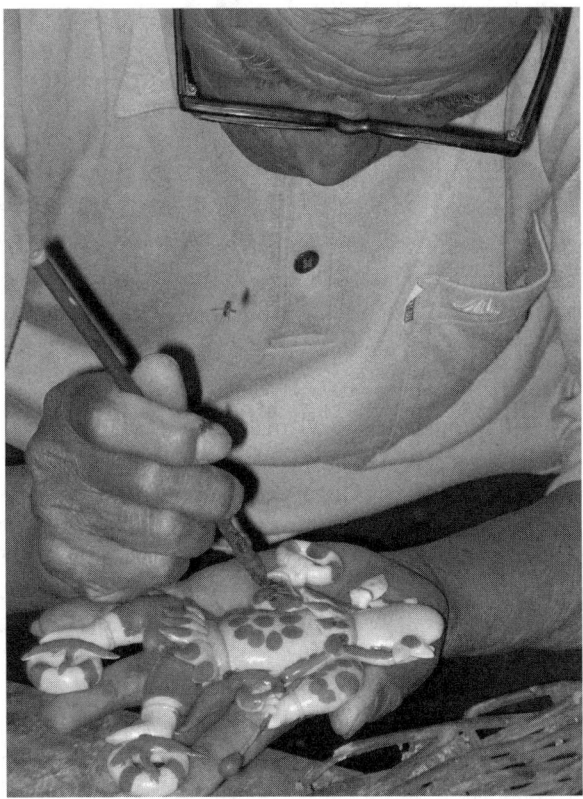

Photograph courtesy of Doug Blandy and ChinaVine

The developers of this animated book initially modified the story's ending in such a way that the wolf did not die from eating the poisoned dough figures, but instead got sick and ran away. The motivations for changing the story's ending were reasonable. The developers of the book wanted to be sensitive to the preservation of wolves as an endangered species in the United States and were concerned that, because children might access the book, killing the wolf may be too disturbing.

In keeping with ChinaVine's partnership methodology, Kristin and I consulted with folklorists and scholars in China on the issue of whether or not the wolf should be killed in *The Wolf and the Dough Children*. In one particular case, a folklorist and folklore students were adamant that the wolf should be killed. In their view, not to kill the wolf would render the tale inauthentic. Given ChinaVine's mission, the research method associated with the project, and the centrality of the tale to the collective identity of Lang Village, the conclusion was changed to the wolf being poisoned to death.

The conversation about killing the wolf was rich, nuanced, and informative. My fieldwork in China introduced me to the complexities associated with the rapid changes currently taking place in China and the effect of these changes on China's traditional cultural heritage. Among the folklorists, artists, and other scholars I have met in China, there is the expressed desire to both protect and simultaneously acknowledge that traditions are evolving. *The Wolf and the Dough Children*, like any example of material culture that is crossing boundaries and contexts, needs to be interrogated fully and openly about the different ideologies and worldviews associated with it as it moves across time, cultures, and contexts.

CONCLUSION

The world is filled with a vast array of cultural expressions unfamiliar to each of us. In some cases, the design, construction, and meaning of certain forms may seem vaguely familiar, but there is an enormous number we know little to nothing about. Items deemed alien to our way of life are often regarded as such because they are fashioned and used by people we do not know and whose values and ways of life we do not fully comprehended. Sometimes, this unfamiliarity can lead us to consider others and their material culture mysterious and exotic, causing us to segregate and isolate ourselves from them. People and their expressions are too often regarded as different, odd, or something to be feared because others are unaccustomed to their presence. To combat this apprehension toward cultural conversance and the all too frequent separation of people and groups from one another, we believe it is through an investigation and understanding of the material culture in people's lives—the expressions made, used, and preserved by others and ourselves—that we begin to sort through and better understand the humanity of those we know little about, whether they reside next door or on the other side of the world.

CHAPTER 5

Technology and Material Culture

Much of what can be considered material culture can also be considered technology. Broadly defined, technology includes, but is not limited to, tools, clothing, art, machines, information systems, the Internet, and even the body. Technology so pervades daily life that periods of history are referenced in terms of technological development. For example, the Stone Age, the Agrarian Age, the Industrial Age, the recent Information Age, and now what some are referring to as the Hybrid Age (Khanna & Khanna, 2011) are all associated with the use of technology during these periods. The Hybrid Age is characterized by ubiquitous computing, intelligent technology, anthropomorphic technology, and the integration of technology across fields for the purpose of creating utilitarian devices, along with the disruption of life at a pace difficult for individuals, society, and culture to accommodate (Khanna & Khanna, 2011). Keeping a broad-based definition of *technology* in mind, consider the following three examples and the material culture associated with each.

The July 7/July 14, 2014, issue of *Time* included a 39-page special report titled "The Smarter Home: The Dwellings of the Future Will Make You Calmer, Safer, Richer and Healthier—and They Already Exist Now." Contributors to this special issue encouraged readers to imagine living in homes that include outdoor spaces that motivate activity, energy efficient and sustainable heating and cooling systems that respond in advance to your preferences, weather tracking systems that also water the lawn, and gardens that ensure good air quality. This special report introduced readers to a variety of everyday gadgets, such as piggy banks, toothbrushes, toys, and audio systems that are "smart" to the extent that they may improve their owner's life through the technology embedded within them. Readers learned of homes that are "recycled," "disaster-proof," include games to encourage good hygiene, and are responsive to physical disabilities to such an extent that many of those disabilities are no longer of consequence (Gibbs, 2014).

Smartphones, within a remarkably short period of time, have become significant tools for making art as well as primary sources for experiencing art. Sometimes referred to as *artphones*, numerous apps are available for creating work in singular and multiple digital media. Museums, such as the Metropolitan Museum of Art in New York City, partner with photographers, using artphones, who roam their galleries, take photographs, and post on social media accounts such as Instagram. Hordes of image-makers are posting their artistry to social media. Professional and everyday critics are commenting on this artistry as well as on art appearing in more traditional settings such as galleries and theaters. Arguably, new genres, such as the ubiquitous "selfie," are arising as a result of the creative attributes of the phone. Even artists who are not working in digital formats can look to digital sounds and images available on phones as sources of inspiration.

If there is any doubt about the extent to which we are tethered to the smartphone/artphone, place yours on a table within easy reach and see how long you can go without accessing it or answering its ring or buzz as you receive social media invites, notifications of new products, current event alerts, phone calls, text messages, and email.

Robotic health-care workers are appearing in hospitals and care facilities. Such devices are dispensing medicine, monitoring vital signs, providing rehabilitation, encouraging social interaction, and offering comfort. Robots are playing sports, and there is now a RoboCup for robotic soccer players. Robotic drones and cars are being seriously considered as home delivery devices. Drones are available to consumers for entertainment or for holding cameras to capture aerial points of view. Scientists are experimenting with robots of limited intelligence that, when paired with hundreds of others and programmed with a specific algorithm, can, as a swarm, create a choreographed routine akin to multicellular organisms and flocks of birds.

Clearly, as the examples above suggest, current technological trends are disrupting traditional conceptions of how technology and humans intersect. People often resist change, and it is not surprising that there is often a lag between the introduction of new technologies, like those described above, and the social and cultural adaptations necessary in order for a technological innovation to be embraced. It is also not surprising that within this volatile environment, people are experiencing anxiety and dissonance. Consider the reactions to the introduction of the Google Glass prototype. These wearable computers accessed the Internet and could record personal encounters through photographs and video. There were reports of them being barred from places of business and recreation as well as legislative initiatives to limit their use. Google Glass was a focus of Stop the Cyborgs (stopthecyborgs.org/), a web-based initiative promoting personal privacy and freedom from government or corporate control. Downloadable signs stating that "Google Glass Is Banned on These Premises" were available on the website for posting. Distribution of the Google Glass prototype was discontinued, with development continuing.

Phillip Vannini (2009) refers to the process of adapting to new technologies as "domestication." He describes domestication as:

> A common concept in technology studies that highlights the growing mutual adaptation of individuals to the design, function, and significance of objects—as well as the shaping of the latter in accordance to the needs and values of the former. . . . Domestication refers to the incorporation of objects in the realm of the mundane . . . the taming of the technologically wild and the cultivation of that which has been tamed. (p. 17)

Because of the ubiquitous nature of technology, a singular theoretical or philosophical approach to technology will not suffice. However, material culture studies does offer possibilities for interrogating the values, attitudes, and beliefs driving technological innovation as well as the resulting material culture shaped by that innovation. Technology, in the broadest sense, as W. David Kingery (1993) observes, has been integral to material culture studies because technology:

> involves the design, creation, distribution, and use of an enormous variety of artifacts. . . . Technology covers the spectrum from continuing, rather dull everyday tasks to esoteric revolutionary innovations [like those described above] affecting humankind's circumstances and behavior. (p. 215)

A material culture studies orientation to technology is particularly helpful in understanding and appreciating the continuous relationship of technology to society and society to technology. Does society determine technology or does technology determine society? As Steven Lubar (1996) argues,

> the details of technological change are merely a means to an end. The end is to better understand some bigger issue, whether it be, on the one hand, cultural change, social change, class, ethnicity, gender, race—the big questions of American history, or, on the other hand, the nature of technological knowledge, the relations of science and technology, or the processes of technological change or technological creativity and design—the key issues of the history of technology. (p. 31)

We agree with John Dewey (1899) on the importance of critically engaging with technology and the social and cultural changes it encourages. The domestication of technology as described above would occur, from a Deweyan perspective, in an environment that is made transparent through citizen engagement. Dewey recognized there is a profound relationship between technology and social change. As a consequence, in order for social change to occur, citizens must understand the influence of technology on society and everyday life. David I. Waddington (2010) has updated Dewey's concept to create an approach he refers to as "critical transparency" (p. 621). His approach, a synthesis of Bruno Latour's view of science as the collective actions of scientists with Dewey's commitment to transparency, "allows citizens to analyze science and technology carefully, while simultaneously taking a watchful stance towards the ramifications of scientific and technological developments" (p. 621). Critical transparency is achieved in education by encouraging "students to inquire about the history and everyday practice of science and technology" and by persuading "students to question the dominant discourses of science and technology" (p. 631). Such an orientation to technology is fully compatible with approaches to technology found in material culture studies. As Lubar (1996) observes:

> Technological artifacts must be considered in the way we consider other aspects of culture—that is, we should look at technological ideas and objects to see how they were made, communicated, and received, the ways in which they set forth meaning and intent, for both the maker and the user. (p. 32)

Because technology has been a longstanding subject of material culture studies, the field provides approaches that assist in rendering technology critically transparent. What follows are six approaches drawn from the literature—systemic, narrative, ethnographic, biographical, a tetrad, and taxonomic. Additional approaches that support a material culture studies orientation are drawn from related fields.

A SYSTEMS APPROACH TO TECHNOLOGY

Kingery (1993) proposes a *systems* approach to the study of technology. He recognizes that people have created and used technology to mediate their relationship with the material environment. Acknowledging the multiplicity of artifacts that have resulted, Kingery argues that these artifacts are best understood if technology is considered "as an interrelated system" (p. 216). Consider, for example, the artphone, introduced earlier in this chapter. Although the artphone could be studied in relation to traditional academic fields such as art, art history, history, or engineering, a more "rational" approach, according to Kingery, is to focus on the larger systems associated with the artphone. The system in which the artphone exists includes the procurement of the materials from which the artphone is made, its design (both aspects of the design that are utilitarian and those that are meant to elicit pleasure), how and where it is manufactured, how it is distributed and the economics of distribution, the characteristics of the public that uses it, how it is perceived by the public, its lifespan in its original form, and possible ways that it could be reused once it has been technologically surpassed and rendered obsolete. Important to this approach is the identification of other systems that intersect with the system in which the artphone exists. Also important to interrogate is the social and cultural context in which the artphone system operates, as well as the values, attitudes, and beliefs driving the creation and use of the artphone. And within a systemic approach, it is essential to study the degree to which the artphone is responding to social and cultural forces, as well as the degree to which the artphone may be changing society and culture.

TECHNOLOGY AND NARRATIVE

Ian Woodward (2009) would argue that the artphone is firmly embedded in culture and represents a cultural category materialized. There is an intimate interrelationship between technological objects and the values, attitudes, and beliefs that they confirm. Woodward, in applying his approach to the iPod, states that "for some people the iPod is a symbol of mobile, aural-aesthetic transcendent pleasure, a precious totem in urban settings" (p. 59). Woodward's poetic description of the iPod exemplifies his belief that it is through narratives, or stories, that objects achieve their power (see Chapter 2). He also believes that narratives are:

> basic structures of everyday perception and action. We use narratives to understand what happens in our own lives, the lives of others, and the world at large. . . . Narratives allow us to piece together events, making sense of disparate experiences, as if they were part of an understandable whole. Importantly, narratives frequently come to life by being embodied in objects. (pp. 59–60)

Using Woodward's (2009) approach, the study of technology requires an examination of the stories that people tell about the meaning and history of an object, as well as the way that people use those stories to reinforce individual or collective identity. Stories about objects do not exist in isolation. As a result, discovering the larger narratives of which such stories are a part is crucial to understanding the larger cultural context. Using the artphone as an example, the stories surrounding the object assist us in understanding the social status of those who use the device, how creativity is facilitated within culture, creativity and mobility, the economics of creativity, and the social networks associated with creativity made possible through the use of an interactive device.

Woodward rightly recognized that technology has enabled objects to tell stories about people. For example, the robotic health-care workers described above are collecting and interpreting information (telling stories) about the people they are serving. The smart homes described above encourage people to perform stories that have been conceived to enhance quality of life. Data collected by a smart home may, in some cases, be accessed later as a story that gauges that quality of life in relationship to some identified norm.

OBJECT ETHNOGRAPHY

Ethnography is a well-known method for studying people and culture. Ethnographic methods assist researchers in experiencing culture from the point of view of those people living within it. Recently, ethnographic methods have been used to illuminate the point of view of material culture. For example, Susan Leigh Star (1999) has written about the importance of applying ethnographic research methods to the study of infrastructure. In doing so, she has studied the archives of the World Health Organization as well as newspaper accounts of racial recategorization under apartheid in South Africa. Inspired by Star, C. W. Anderson, Juliette De Maeyer, and Heather Ford (2013) presented a series of ethnographic studies of objects on the website Ethnography Matters. These studies were organized around the question "What can we gain from an ethnography of objects—especially in the fields of technology, media, and journalism research?" Hyperlinks, Wikipedia bots, and faked 19th-century photographs were among the objects studied. Elsewhere on Ethnography Matters, Ford (2012) interviewed Stuart Geiger about his research applying ethnographic methods to the study of robotic experience and the controversy associated with applying "culture" to nonhuman societies. Victoria Carrington (2012), recognizing that youth live a polymediated life and that "an artifact and the individuals who use it co-construct lived experience through their everyday interactions" (p. 28), studied a young woman's iPhone and its use within youth culture. For Carrington, "Object ethnographies . . . are nested analyses that build a rich analysis of the interaction between artifact and user in the creation and experience of everyday life" (p. 28).

Luke Eric Lassiter (2004) has proposed a collaborative ethnographic method for working with members of communities and cultures. Lassiter promotes this method as one way to try to achieve a correct interpretation, representation, or description of people and their cultural groups. In Lassiter's view, noncollaborative methods invite misrepresentation. It is intriguing to consider applying his research method to objects. To do so would involve the following four steps from Lassiter with our adaptations in brackets below.

1. participating in the lives of others [objects] (which may include learning a new language—[for example, computer programming language, emoticons, emojis] or learning how to behave appropriately [with objects] within a particular setting);

2. observing behavior [of objects, including interactions between objects and the people who use them];
3. taking fieldnotes (which may include jotting down first impressions, drawing maps, or writing extensive descriptions of [objects] cultural scenes); and
4. conducting interviews [with users of objects as well as objects themselves if they are responsive hardware or software] (which may include both informal conversations and more formal exchanges). (p. 2)

THE BIOGRAPHY OF THINGS

Closely aligned with object ethnography is doing biographies of things. Igor Kopytoff (1986) believes that objects or things live lives, much as people do, and that these lives can be communicated through biography. Kopytoff is an anthropologist and believes strongly that biographies of things must be communicated within a cultural context. Referencing the use of biography within anthropology, Kopytoff (1986) argues that the application of such an approach as applied to humans can also be applied to things:

> In doing the biography of a thing, one would ask questions similar to those one asks about people:
>
> What, sociologically, are the biographical possibilities inherent in its "status" and in the period and culture, and how are these possibilities realized?
>
> Where does the thing come from and who made it? What has been its career so far, and what do people consider to be an ideal career for such a thing?
>
> What are the recognized "ages" or periods in the things "life," and what are the cultural markers for them?
>
> How does the thing's use change with its age, and what happens to it when it reaches the end of usefulness? (pp. 66–67)

A Teachers Guide: Exploring Material Culture in the Classroom, published by PBS on the Internet (www.pbs.org/wgbh/roadshow/teachers_intheclassroom.html), provides a framework through which the biography of a thing can be compiled. Consider this framework in relationship to the artphone described earlier in the chapter. A biography of an artphone would begin by examining the object itself or images and narratives about the object and produced by the object. Discovering what the object is made of is important. The next step would be to research the artphone to ascertain information about the design and use of the item, as well as information about any precedents leading up to its creation. Important to the artphone's biography is its economic value and the determination of that value. How does one come to own an artphone? What are the ideals, attitudes, and beliefs associated with the artphone, as expressed by those who use it as well as those who are challenged by its capabilities? How do artphones exemplify our times? Once this initial analysis takes place, the next step is to engage with Kopytoff's (1986) questions, in the quote above, to create a biography of the thing.

THE TETRAD

Marshall McLuhan (McLuhan & McLuhan, 1988) designed a teaching tool for analyzing media that can also be applied to the study of technology. Referred to as the *tetrad of media effects*, McLuhan's tool poses questions that divide the effects of media on society by four. McLuhan's tetrad is depicted as five connecting diamonds that form an "X" with the media or technology in the center. Questions associated with the other four diamonds are as follows:

- What does the medium [technology] enhance?
- What does the medium [technology] make obsolete?
- What does the medium [technology] retrieve that had been obsolesced earlier?
- What does the medium [technology] flip into when pushed to extremes?

McLuhan's tetrad, when applied to the artphone, would reveal the following:

- The artphone enhances the creative process through mobile digital interactive technology.
- The artphone renders obsolete the place-bound digital device used for creative activity.
- The artphone retrieves mobility as integral to the creative process as facilitated through digital devices.
- The artphone flips into an interactive social network of creatives.

For McLuhan, and in keeping with Dewey (1899), what the tetrad of media effects makes possible is to bring transparency to the relationship between technology and culture. Use of the tetrad of media effects is, in and of itself, a creative act. Though the application of the tetrad of media effects to the artphone above may resonate with some readers, other readers may disagree and apply the tetrad to the artphone with different results.

THE TAXONOMY OF THE SENSORIUM

Earlier in this chapter there was the suggestion that we currently live in the Hybrid Age—an age characterized by the intersection of the body and technology. David Rose (2014), though not explicitly referring to a Hybrid Age, does believe we are situated in a transformative moment in which human desire is behind the development of an "Internet of Things." In this Internet, the plethora of everyday objects that surround us are computerized to respond to, predict, and shape our desires while simultaneously being linked through a vast electronic network. Rose (2014) refers to such objects as being "enchanted"—enchanted, in that technology has the capability of infusing "ordinary things with a bit of magic to create more satisfying interaction and evoke an emotional response" (p. 13). For Rose, this is one technological trajectory among four that are likely to coexist. The other three trajectories Rose proposes are associated with *terminals*—ubiquitous embedded pixilated screens (think smartphones and tablets), *prosthetics* or wearable technology, and *animism*—animated (robotic) friends and assistants.

Critical methods for living in the Hybrid Age are only just beginning to emerge. Artists often act as cultural seers, and it is not surprising that artists are providing early approaches to living within, critiquing, and shaping the Hybrid Age. In this regard, the book *Sensorium: Embodied Experience, Technology, and Contemporary Art* catalogs and expands upon a groundbreaking, prescient, and provocative 2006–2007 exhibit at the MIT List Visual Arts Center (Jones, 2006). Experiencing the *Sensorium* as an exhibit required the use of all five senses. This challenged the prominence of the visual—the sense that one usually associates with art exhibits. The example that follows, from the exhibit and book, cannot possibly represent the whole, but it does provide some indication of how an artist responded to the exhibit's purpose.

François Roche and his conceptual architectural firm R&Sie(n) are based in France. Bruce Sterling (2012), in a *Wired* profile aptly titled "An Architect's Wet-Cement Dream: Just as Termites Build Castles on Earth, Robots Could Erect Skyscrapers on the Moon," describes Roche as "exploring what happens when the usual constraints are allowed to fall away and things get wild and loose." Sterling goes on to describe architectural projects, called "viabs," in which a building conforms to its inhabitants' "needs and desires." Such structures "are not set and specific, but impermanent and malleable—merely viable—made of uniform, recyclable substances like adobe . . . a great rotting blooming stony bubble of a building . . . unplanned, responsive, densely monitored, massively customized, and rock solid, with all modern conveniences" (Sterling, 2012).

For *Sensorium*, Roche proposed an experience about sustainability designed to "provide a phobic response" (Farver, 2006, p. 87). MITea, an inflatable tearoom, would invite visitors to partake of tea knowing the quality of the water used to brew it. The water used to make the tea would be "reinvested" purified water from rain, melting snow, MIT's toilets, and waste system. Roche's installation asks, "Will visitors to the exhibit be willing to taste tea made with MIT's wastewater? Will knowledge of the tea's source create paranoia, changing how it will taste? Will this effect on the senses then overcome good sense and keep people from drinking it?" (Farver, 2006, p. 87).

Jones (2006) offers a system of organization designed to assist in understanding the work of an artist's, such as Roche's, relations with technology:

Immersive

the "cave" paradigm: the virtual helmet, the black box video, the earphone set

Alienated

taking technology and "making it strange," exaggerating attributes to provoke shock, using technologies to switch senses or induce disorientation

Interrogative

work that repurposes or remakes devices to enhance their insidious or wondrous properties; available data translated into sensible systems

Residual

work that holds on to an earlier technology, repurposes or even fetishizes an abandoned one

Resistant

work that refuses to use marketed technologies for their stated purpose; work that pushes viewers to reject technologies or subvert them

Adaptive

work that takes up technologies and extends or applies them for creative purposes, producing new subjects for the technologies in question. (p. 6)

Despite the abstractness of this taxonomy, it does assist in considering the overall experience provided by a technology, technology as it disrupts the everyday, critically engaging with technology, discovering the remnants of past technology within contemporary technology, and repurposing technology. Jones's (2006) position is that technological enhancements "no longer provoke . . . apocalyptic excitement. . . . The relative calm this situation provides gives us time for reflection: a propitious moment for artists and other culture workers to interpret, think, and reckon with the *sense* of our mediated sensorium" (p. 5). Her taxonomy begins to suggest ways to navigate and make sense of technology, and contributes to critically transparent interactions with technology as it is manifesting today.

VIDEOGAMES AND VIRTUAL ENVIRONMENTS

What has yet to be considered in this chapter are videogames and virtual environments such as *Second Life*. Both reinforce the connection between technology and the multisensory body. These are experimental environments in which people can create and test digital personas distinguishable or indistinguishable from their analog selves. Questions arise about the relationship between the analog flesh-and-blood self and the disembodied digital self. How does one inform the other? How do the sociocultural contexts of each interrelate? When does one's self take precedence over the other? What occurs when one's analog self interacts with another's digital self and vice versa?

Ethnographic approaches, including Lassiter's (2004) collaborative approach as described above, can be used to study virtual environments, including videogames, and the people who inhabit them. In addition, there is a growing body of scholarly literature directed toward analyses of videogames, as well as critiques offered by users, designers, developers, and journalists associated with game criticism.

Game designer Daniel Cook (2011), in classifying the types of game criticism, suggests a series of questions that can be used to critique a game or virtual environment:

- What is the emotional experience associated with playing through a game?
- What is the impact of the game on the player and the player's culture?
- How does the game connect with ongoing questions in the arts, history, literature, and philosophy?
- How does the game reflect trends in the industry?
- Would you recommend this game to others?

KirbyKid (2008), in a "how to" on writing a critical videogame review, encourages additional questions:

- How is the game paced?
- How difficult is the game and what contributes to the difficulty?
- How do the game elements come together in support of the experience of the game?
- How is play controlled?
- What is the game's story, theme, plot, interactive plot line, visuals, scene construction, and characters?
- How intuitive is the game?
- Are the elements of the game effectively balanced?

Any study of a game should include an analysis of the game's gender politics. For example, Anita Sarkeesian's (n.d.) blog examines the representation of women in videogames. Through a series of videos, *Tropes vs. Women in Video Games*, Sarkeesian examines "the plot devices and patterns most often associated with female characters in gaming." Tropes include women as background, the Ms. Male character, and damsel in distress. The blog suggests questions such as the following for critiquing games:

- How are women represented in the game?
- How are men represented in the game?
- What are the similarities and differences in the way that men and women are represented?
- Does the game encourage gender stereotypes?

However, Sarkeesian's project goes beyond the representation of women. It suggests that a critique of videogames and virtual environments from a feminist perspective must also take into consideration race, ethnicity, ability, and sexuality, and age, among other attributes used to oppress others (see Huntermann, n.d.)

CONCLUSION

This chapter introduced readers to the important place that technology has had within the history of material culture studies. Material culture studies and related fields have much to offer in critically examining current and emerging technologies. Approaches introduced in this chapter can assist in promoting the critical transparency necessary to educate people about technology, society, and culture, aiding in the exploration of material culture from the past, as well as those forms of material culture that will emerge in the years ahead.

CHAPTER 6

Multisensory Art, Artists, and Art Education

Art and material culture are very blended in their study, as art is a form of material culture. Art is not situated outside or above the territory of material culture, holding a revered place of separation and hierarchical distinction over it. Rather, the opposite is actually the case, as it is under the extensive umbrella of material culture that art resides. Art, like all human constructs, reflects the values, beliefs, understandings, and actions of the maker/performer, and serves as a window into the life and social, psychological, and intellectual context surrounding this individual. However, the same can be said of all makers and performers, whether or not these people are considered to be artists. Thus, the exploration and understanding of material culture aligns itself in very accordant ways with the investigation of art, artists, and all makers and performers. For this reason, it is important that art educators explore deeply the past, present, and future worlds of art within the study of material culture.

SUPERIORITY GIVEN THE VISUAL

For the past 400 years or more, the art world has held the sense of sight in highest regard. Artworks are viewed, inspected, seen, scanned, beheld, observed, looked at, and gazed upon—all acts of visual characterization. We call what artists do "visual art," not as a description of the most immediate sense by which art is generated (primarily with our hands), but instead to indicate the sensory organ we have customarily utilized in our response to it. Museum walls are filled with objects and images we are called upon to address through visual means; thus, visitors to museums are regarded quite often through a sight-based nomenclature: the *viewer*.

Through the years, art has been marked by change. Emerging artistic styles have replaced those of previous generations with an ever-expanding array of possibilities for creative involvement. For instance, the sculptural artist Alexander Calder shook up the art world in radical ways by the addition of movement to his work. Lightweight sculptural pieces were suspended in galleries, and these ethereal forms rotated in response to visitor movement and circulating air currents. However, as innovative as Calder's works were to viewers in the 1930s and more recent years, they are still regarded primarily as visual engagements. The works of notable artists such as Pablo Picasso, Georgia O'Keeffe, Frida Kahlo, and Andy Warhol were powerful and influential when they flashed into the artworld, yet it is useful to remember that the multitude of innovative art objects of these makers is still primarily visual in form. Most encounters with the art of these individuals were then and continue to be regarded as a visual experience.

Moreover, as we move beyond museum walls and into the surrounding world of life today, we are bombarded with a vast array of images, objects, and expressions. These are what many writers have termed *visual culture*. According to art educators Terry Barrett (2003), David Darts (2004), Paul Duncum (2006), Kerry Freedman (2003), Karen Keifer-Boyd and Jane Maitland-Gholson (2007), Kevin Tavin (2003), Pam Taylor (2007), and many others, the expansive list of visual culture includes things such as shopping malls, fast-food restaurants, television programs, movies and CDs, computer games, and toy and furniture design, among a vast host of similar expressions found in the world around us. This wide and diverse set of visual culture references raises a perplexing question while at the same time demonstrating the power of the visual in our lives today: With the range of all the senses (touch, smell, sound, taste, and sight) that we use to engage with these ubiquitous objects and purposed spaces in our contemporary world, why are they referred to as *visual* culture? In many such expressions of visual culture, the aspect of sight is one feature but may not be its primary characteristic, yet the term *visual* is still used to describe them. Utilizing this descriptor demonstrates sight's highly ingrained and unequivocal acceptance as acting above the other senses activated by these objects, spaces, and expressions. But why is this so? Why do we call certain things and spaces visual culture when in actuality there are multiple senses vigorously involved in a person's use of and experience with them? Longstanding Western tradition has emphasized the precedence of sight over the other physical senses, and we continue these habitual practices today through our customary use of language and familiar terminology.

Yes, the eyes have it! They are considered the most prominent of the human senses and have been the focus (intentional use) of our sensory attention in the world and art for centuries. But what about the other senses? Are they inherently inferior to the eye? Is the sense of smell subordinate to that of sight? Are taste and hearing of less import than seeing? Is touch of smaller worth than sight? Has our vision always been regarded as the most prominent organ of the senses, or have we become so attuned to our sense of sight, over time and particularly most recently, that the other senses have lost their comparative import?

What would our world be like if we had a greater vocabulary for cataloging smells, other than referring to them in metaphoric terms such as smelling like a rose or having the odor of a rotten egg? What if we as individuals spent as much time centering on the world of taste as we do on the world of sight? We have learned to discriminate tremendous subtleties and nuances of vision (we now have given nomenclature to thousands of colors), but our vocabulary for identifying and differentiating tastes is fairly limited, with the primary flavor responses of sweet, sour, salty, pungent, bitter, and astringent. As art educators, we believe it is a useful and necessary exercise to pause and reflect on the language used to describe our response to the wide range of objects, images, and expressions that surround us in the world and art world today. Doing so will challenge us and our students to think deeply about the use of language and the primacy given to the visual in our lives.

MULTISENSORY ART AND ARTISTS

Our appeal for art educators to pay greater attention to the complete range of senses occurs in response to the expanding presence of multisensory artistic activity. For the past half-century in particular, and increasingly in the past 2 decades, artists are demonstrating growing involvement with the complete span of senses in their art. Contemporary works of art are burgeoning beyond the realm of sight, as artists employ smell, sound, touch, and even taste in their work. Visual art, in many instances, is transitioning into what may be more appropriately termed *multisensory engagement*, where viewers of art are aptly described as *participants in* or *companions with* the art. This shift in the character of art and the relationship among artist, art, and perceiver alters the fundamental nature of what has long been termed *visual art*, and also brings with it a new set of conversations in our analysis, interpretation, and discussion of these artworks.

This is not to imply that the shift in the art world toward a multisensory engagement sprang to life within the past few years. Such multiformed sense-based expressive activity has had a sporadic yet clearly building presence in art for some time. The Dadaists, whose manifestations in various forms of visual art, literature, and theater embraced the senses of sight, sound, touch, and sometimes smell, took an antiwar political stance toward World War I through forms of expression that ran counter to conventional art of the time. Dada artists laid the groundwork for a wide range of exploratory artistic expressions that would follow. The experimental music of John Cage, introduced during the

1950s, was coupled with the ideas and found art of Marcel Duchamp and the avant-garde sound and sight performances of Joseph Beuys in the 1960s and that of his associate Nam June Paik, as George Maciunas and Fluxus emerged as an international network of artists in Europe and the United States in the late 1950s and 1960s. At the same time, Allan Kaprow's unscripted "Happenings" captured the attention of the world and art world and became a foundation for the performance art that followed. The activities of these and other groundbreaking artists challenged the established and familiar notions of art, as their products were complex and diverse forms of artistic expression, with most being multisensory in composition.

Since the 1960s, an increasing number of artists have experimented with and embraced a wide range of sensory interrogation and activity in their work. Artistic investigations through the use of smell, sound, touch, taste, and sight are increasing rapidly, and provide an intriguing look at the range of involvement that art may play in everyday life. What follows here is a brief look at the work of 10 artists or artistic teams who explore the senses that are often neglected: smell, touch, sound, and taste. The number of examples included here is limited and the discussions are meant only as an introduction to these artists and their work. Restricted also in this book format is access to the rich sensory experience encountered through direct participation with these works. Such are the limits of early-21st-century publishing and sensory access. In the future, much greater accessibility and presentation of all sensory modes will undoubtedly be available. In the meantime, readers are urged to explore these specific works of art online in conjunction with reading the following synopses about these works and their makers.

Readers are also encouraged to delve further into the lives and work of these artists, as well as to explore online resources for the many other multisensory artists not mentioned here. At the end of this chapter, we also provide a list of additional multisensory artists and curators, virtual and physical sites referring to multisensory art, and events and exhibitions of a multisensory nature.

TEN ARTISTS/ARTISTIC TEAMS WHOSE WORK TRANSCENDS THE VISUAL

1. Edward Kienholz, *The State Hospital* (1966)

Edward Kienholz's installation *The State Hospital* is perplexing at first look. The exterior is a large white box (8 by 12 by 10 feet), showing a locked door with a small barred window at approximate eye level. The sign "WARD 19" painted in the upper corner to the left of the door projects the aura of an institutional setting rather than a jail. A look inside beyond the bars of the door reveals a disturbing sight: Two nearly identical male figures lie naked on stark metal bunk beds, with the pose of each echoing the other. Each man extends prone on what appears to be a filthy mattress. The arms of both figures are manacled to the bed frame with leather straps. Both men have heads formed from fishbowls. The figure prone on the top bed is surrounded by a red oval neon tube, constructed in the manner of a speech balloon from a comic strip. Through this, a sense of self-reflection by the lower figure is conveyed. The room is lit by a single uncovered light bulb hanging from the center of the ceiling. A bedpan rests on the floor, beyond the reach of either restrained figure. More than a nauseous sculptural expression for the eyes, Kienholz has added another sensory dimension to this piece. When the work was first displayed at the Los Angeles County Museum in 1966, Kienholz included the smell of institutional disinfectant or, as Janson (1991) has written, "A sickly hospital smell" (p. 775). In this way, the olfactory and visual aspects of the piece work in tandem to produce and reinforce the artist's stark message of human isolation, cruelty, and suffering.

2. Bridget Baker, *So It Goes* (1996)

Bridget Baker is a South African artist who has utilized the sense of smell in her work. Through her installations and other art forms, Baker has investigated events from her childhood as she acknowledges that smell and memory are reciprocal and persistently entwined. Baker's 1996 work *So It Goes* is simple in format but complex in response. The work consists of four small tin containers (3.5 by 2 centimeters each) positioned a few inches apart on a pedestal. Situated inside at the bottom of each container is a photograph of Baker and her father, taken not long before his death from a heart attack when Bridget was 5 years old. She has no immediate recollections of her father, only secondhand stories and this one photograph, which has been reproduced four times here—one photo for each tin. Placed in the tins, on top of each photograph, are various amounts of aromatically pungent Vicks® VapoRub, obscuring more or less of the photograph in each container. Together, these visual and olfactory offerings in each tin create a dilemma for anyone experiencing them. The visitor is drawn close to the work, in order to see the small and partially obscured photograph at the bottom of each tin, yet they are repelled from getting too close to the image by the powerful odor of the analgesic balm. Baker's multisensory work here acts as an intriguing site of tension between the sensory features of sight and smell.

3. Iain Mott and Marc Raszewski, *Summoned Voices* (2003)

The 2003 exhibition *Summoned Voices* served as an auditory repository and playback of people's recorded sound expressions. This cooperative installation by Iain Mott and Marc Raszewski consisted of a series of door installations, each with an intercom that visitors were encouraged to use in the recording of voice or sound. Participants to the exhibit were invited to speak, exude sounds, generate noises, or sing into the active intercom in each door, where these sounds were then recorded. The recording system for each intercom was connected to a computer. Each participant's recording was stored within the computer for the duration of the exhibit. Thus, in a collaborative manner, the voices and sounds of previous participants were heard in response to and in association with those who engaged with the intercom recording later. Together, the recorded and played voices and auditory emissions became an amalgamation of sounds made over time, a record of community expression within a context of anticipation and wonder. As a work of art, *Summoned Voices* has as much to do with a sound experience, initiated with the touch of an intercom button, as it does with its visual qualities.

4. Carsten Höller, *Test Site* (2007)

Test Site (2007) was one of many Carsten Höller's works exploring the confluence of experimentation and play. As Höller's seventh commission in his "Unilever Series," this sculpture was installed in Turbine Hall at London's Tate Modern between October 2006 and April 2007 and consisted of five indoor slides: two initiated on the second floor, and one slide each on the third, fourth, and fifth floors. Each slide terminated on the first floor of the museum. The slides were tubular in form, constructed of stainless steel and fiberglass, and ranged from 52 to 190 feet in length. Since 1998, working with slides has been an ongoing project for Höller. In each case, the slides are impressive sculptures to be viewed, and someone does not need to accelerate down the fiberglass tube to appreciate the work. However, these kinesthetically purposed objects do challenge the traditional beliefs and standards of what is encountered in most art museums, where visitors are generally instructed not to handle the art. In this case, visitors to the museum are given permission not only to touch the work but to participate with it in a somewhat daring and thrilling manner.

5. Ernesto Neto, *Multisensory Biomorphic Sculpture* (Since the late 1980s)

The Brazilian artist Ernesto Neto is, without question, one of the most intriguing multisensory artists working today. Neto's vast walkthrough installations consist of huge sheets or tubular containers of translucent Lycra stretched from ceiling to floor in diagonal directions, or oversized bulbous Lycra bags suspended from the ceiling. These fabric containers are often loaded with many pounds of ground spices and fragrant plants such as cinnamon, clove, lavender, turmeric, or pepper, which are used to secure the sculptures to the floor or, when suspended, to scent the surrounding air as visitors move around them. These sculptural pieces are often immense and visually captivating works of art, yet they have as much to do with the visitor engaging the various pungent smells of spices or plants as they do with encountering these works visually. Many of Neto's artworks involve the sense of touch as well. His tunnel-like Lycra sculptural containers project the notion of giant organic membranes that beckon visitors to come near and enter. When visitors do so, they soon learn that the containers require guests to maneuver through the Lycra fabric actively using feet and arms, much like swimming through the fabric. Neto's works are filled with surprise and wonder as they provide a sensory experience that embraces in direct ways the senses of smell, touch, and sight.

6. Tony Oursler, "Dolls and Dummies" (Series Begun in the Early 1990s)

Since the early 1990s, Tony Oursler has been combining theatrical-like dummies or dolls with video and sound to form animated works of art that are unmistakably his creations. In these works, Oursler uses trousers and shirts or blouses to delineate human figures, most of them life-sized. To each of the figures Oursler attaches a smooth orbed head constructed of fabric, much like an oval pillow. The head of each figure then takes on human form through a videotape of a talking face that is projected on the rounded surface of the fabric. In this way, the characters are fashioned from cloth, but seem to be alive. The results of Oursler's efforts are often both fascinating and disconcerting. Oursler frequently arranges these figures in positions of unnerving constraint and seemingly painful articulation, sometimes squeezed under heavy furniture and mattresses or emerging from overly confined spaces such as suitcases and storage trunks. Through these video projections, lasting up to 60 minutes, figures speak miserably of their morbid circumstances. Facial expressions and voices call out to visitors for help, telling of their distressing predicament, and sometimes confront those around them with looks of anguish and words of distain. There are instances when the figures project laughter, but not the kind that is returned with delight. Oursler's unsettling figures express through the fusion of sight and sound a world of human lament that causes reflection into our own lives and the core of our condition.

7. Jean-Pierre Gauthier, *Battements et Papillons* (2006)

Canadian artist Jean-Pierre Gauthier combines movement with sound in his 2006 work, *Battements et Papillons*. This technological innovation is an interactive piece, where the movements made by visitors in the exhibition space help determine the sounds emitted from the installation. Comprised of a piano and its bench, aluminum tape, motion detectors, microcontrollers, solenoids, relays, metal tension cables, a motor, and various other objects, *Battements et Papillons* is part of the permanent collection of the Musée d'art contemporain de Montréal. The piece is intriguing yet very straightforward at first encounter, consisting of a large piano and bench covered in aluminum foil. Further inspection of the work reveals much more. The piano and bench are connected through specially designed rods and cables. Motion detectors situated at the corners of the piano bench capture visitors' movement in the space around the piano. These motion detectors then activate four microcontrollers that send digitally coded signals to the relays. Through this technology, the piano keys and primary pedal are then depressed, producing a range of sounds and melodies. However, the piano stays silent when the visitor does not move. Through this interactive piece, those in the space become part of the installation, controlling in measure the sounds emitted by the work of art.

8. Félix González-Torres, "Untitled" *(Portrait of Ross in L.A.)* (1991)

Félix González-Torres's innovative work *"Untitled" (Portrait of Ross in L.A.)* (1991) exemplifies a number of similar installations introduced by the artist in early 1990s. Many of these works have been reproduced multiple times since then. *"Untitled" (Portrait of Ross in L.A.)* is a metaphoric representation of the artist's partner, Ross Laycock, who died of an AIDS-related illness the same year this work was first exhibited (1991). The installation, like many of González-Torres's other works, is politically charged and consists of piles of brightly wrapped, small hard candies. In the case of *"Untitled" (Portrait of Ross in L.A.)*, the installation is comprised of 175 pounds of wrapped candy pieces piled in the corner of the exhibition space. The weight of the candy corresponds to Laycock's body weight when he was healthy. Visitors to the exhibit are encouraged to take a piece of candy from the installation and experience the work by way of touch, taste, and sight. Through the ingestion of the candy, the sculptural installation becomes a part of the visitor, making her or him a living reliquary to both life and death. The diminishing amount of candy in the exhibition over time is meant to symbolize Ross's gradual weight loss in the time leading up to his death. González-Torres specified that the pile of wrapped candy should be regularly brought back to its original weight, thus symbolizing the lastingness of life. The artist continued to make similar installation pieces of wrapped candy intended to be eaten and contemplated until his death in 1996.

9. Antony Gormley, *Blind Light* (2007)

Visitors who step inside Antony Gormley's 28-by-32-by10-foot-6-inch glass box, a work titled *Blind Light*, are enveloped in a swirling cloud of damp fog so dense, they can see only a few inches ahead. The fine fog mist is bright white in color, a hue created by overhead fluorescent lights. Maneuvering within this completely contained and difficult-to-navigate space invokes an array of reactions, ranging from distressing anxiety to expressive euphoria. Inside the enclosure is a completely surrounded tactile and psychologically challenging experience, as one is easily disoriented within the immense fog-shrouded environment. It is difficult—if not impossible—to see others in this space, yet one is decidedly cautious of their potential presence and thus careful not to move too quickly or reach too far for fear of physically encountering an unseen visitor. People emerge from the fog and, within a moment, are enveloped back into it. Some visitors to *Blind Light* find the immersive experience disturbing or constrictive, as the room has only one small passageway in and out, which is impossible to identify until you are inches from it. For this reason, a precautionary notice to the exhibition states: "Visitors with asthma, claustrophobia, or of a nervous disposition are advised to exercise caution when entering." This is, indeed, a useful but not often seen warning about our encounters with art.

10. Kate Goodwin, "Sensing Spaces: Architecture Reimagined" (2014)

In spring 2014, curator Kate Goodwin transformed London's Royal Academy of Arts into a sensing space where architecture was encountered in a challenging and reflective manner. Goodwin's purpose for the exhibition "Sensing Spaces: Architecture Reimagined" was to assist visitors in experiencing architecture's inherently, but often ignored, vast range of sensory elements. Seven architectural projects, created by a collection of international architects or architecture firms, were exhibited within 23,000 square feet of the Royal Academy of Arts in London. In so doing, each project gave attention to structure as experienced through touch, sound, scent, and sight. The Royal Academy of Arts website provides a multimedia overview of Goodwin's curatorial purpose as well as information on the spaces created and those who fashioned them. The intent of the exhibition was to bring architecture to the forefront of people's lives in new and thoughtful ways. Installations were available for visitors to encounter through the entire sweep of the senses, and offered participants an array of reflective opportunities by way of firsthand experience with these architectural installations. Through this exhibition, it was Goodwin's desire for people to take their experience with these multisensory spaces beyond the walls of the Royal Academy, and to consider the impact of architecture on our lives each day.

There appears to be an increase in the number and scope of multisensory artists working today. Beyond the artists discussed to this point, what follows are additional multisensory artists/curators, virtual/physical sites, and events/exhibitions students and teachers are urged to explore, providing a starting place for investigations into dynamic contemporary art practice.

ADDITIONAL MULTISENSORY ARTISTS/CURATORS, VIRTUAL/PHYSICAL SITES, AND EVENTS/EXHIBITIONS READERS ARE URGED TO EXPLORE

Multisensory Artists/Curators

Alice Bradshaw
Peter De Cupere
Jim Drobnick
Olafur Eliasson
Fritz Haeg
Naomi Kendrick
Rafael Lozano-Hemmer
Oswaldo Maciá
Kate McLean, *Sensory Maps*
Jeffrey Shaw, *The Legible City*
Rirkrit Tiravanija
Sissel Tolaas
tobias c. van Veen

Virtual/Physical Sites About Multisensory Art

Art Gallery of Ontario, Multisensory Tours
The Institute for Art and Olfaction
Life in Scents
Museum of Contemporary Rubbish
Olfactive: The Source for Scent Culture
Sensory Sites

Multisensory Art Events/Exhibitions

"Art Out of Sight: The Future of Multisensory Art"
"Down to Earth: Artists Create Edible Landscapes" Schuyllkill Center Second Site

"The Library of Cynicism: The Archaeology of Sound and Smell"
"Olfaction Exhibition"
"Out of Sight! Art of the Senses"
"Sense of Space: A Multi-Sensory Performance by Deafblind Artists"

MULTISENSORY ART AND ART EDUCATION

The increasing exploration of multisensory art has implications for art education. What, specifically, might this inclusion mean for the field? If art education embraces participation with the world of multisensory art, then longstanding and traditional ways of discussing works of art, carrying out instruction in art, and displaying artworks will require reappraisal and, likely, significant change. How should the field of art education and art educators respond to this growing presence of multisensory art? We believe, at the very least, it is our responsibility to provide learners with information about multisensory artists and the changing nature of contemporary art so that students are able to explore such ideas in their own artmaking in ways that are thoughtful and informed. Moreover, as educators, we should share with our students a new and expanding vocabulary that enables them to comprehend the senses more fully and possess the skills necessary to discuss these sensory characteristics in relation to the art they make and embrace.

Beyond the curricular content changes, there would need to be shifts made in art instruction. Multisensory artists are drawn from a vast array of fields and experience, including the sciences, electronics, mechanics, psychology, technology, music, sound study, olfactory investigations, and much more. For this reason, involvement in multisensory art instruction will require art educators to engage in cross-disciplinary investigation and collaborations that take us beyond the traditional manifestations frequently found in visual art. Art instruction would not occur as the isolated field it is often regarded to be.

A shift in art education toward multisensory art involvement would require the employment of instructional materials that are different from what is found in most art classrooms today. It is intriguing to ask: What would an art supply catalog then contain? Would it be filled with items such as paints, paintbrushes, paper, pencils, clay, paste, and other supplies currently found in catalogs? Or would it present a much richer array of materials, including spices and other forms of fragrance, electronic supplies, computer gadgetry, machine apparatus, noise-generating instruments, soundboards, and fog machines? Moreover, how would instruction in art change with the presence of this broad array of equipment and materials? Would teachers and students be called upon to work in greater collaboration with one another, perhaps with other members of their school staff, and in additional educational locations?

Greater community participation may be called for in order for students to achieve success with ideas and materials that are not familiar to them.

Directing attention to the study of multisensory art requires that current strategies for *looking* at art be expanded to embrace a wide variety of ways to encounter works of art beyond sight. Material culture studies, because of its broad framework and inclusive nature, provides useful analytical applications and approaches for accomplishing a more holistic investigation of multisensory art. Within the pages of this book, and particularly in the chapter that follows, is a spectrum of strategies and approaches for analyzing human-formed objects, environments, and expressions drawn from the fields of anthropology, museum studies, popular culture, American studies, folklore, history, environmental aesthetics, and art history. Many of these investigative approaches are beneficial in the study of material culture and will also assist art educators in the analysis of multisensory art. For this reason, readers are encouraged to explore the analytic approaches and strategies offered here and select those most beneficial to them for the study and analysis of multisensory art and all forms of material culture.

CHAPTER 7

Conclusion
Strategies and Approaches for Teaching About and Studying Material Culture

Throughout the book, there is reference to various instructional activities we have used with a wide spectrum of students (K–16) in diverse learning contexts (schools, museums, community locations). Beyond providing pedagogical information periodically within the pages of the book, in bringing this volume to a close, this chapter furnishes 10 additional instructional strategies that we have used with a variety of learners in a range of settings. In addition, this chapter also contains 10 approaches to the study of material culture that we have gleaned from writers in various fields such as art history, anthropology, museum studies, material culture studies, popular culture, and environmental aesthetics. We encourage educators to utilize one or more of these approaches as they and their students explore the rich and vibrant world of material culture.

Setting out to explore the place and potential of material culture within the field of art education, we have introduced a range of ideas and approaches for doing so here. By focusing on topics such as the importance of memory; the political nature of objects; the entwined nature of people, objects, and stories; the power of collecting and collections; the impact of technology within the study of material culture; and the work of multisensory artists, among many other considerations, we desire for you to utilize these ideas and approaches in your work with learners. We believe the study of objects and their power and meaning within our lives holds great potential for fascinating and worthwhile investigation into self and society.

TEN INSTRUCTIONAL STRATEGIES TO USE WITH STUDENTS

The following are 10 specific strategies the authors have developed that educators and learners may use for exploring objects and the value these things hold in our lives.

Instructional Strategy 1: Do I Collect? If So, What Do I Collect and Why?

Many people collect things. Some people collect coins, while others collect Barbie dolls, Impressionist paintings, baseball cards, comic books, matchbooks, ticket stubs, or movie memorabilia. There is a seemingly endless list of what is collected by people throughout our world. Scholarship associated with collecting describes the ubiquitous phenomenon across cultural groups, age groups, gender, history, and motivation. The psychology of collecting has been studied, as have the ways in which collecting enhances one's social standing.

Collecting as a pedagogical approach has also been considered. In this regard, ask students to bring to class one or more examples of things they collect. Students should be prepared to show their object(s), to discuss why they collect these objects, and to answer questions about the collection. If students do not collect anything specific or do not care to share with the class what they collect, they can be asked to bring an example of something they know others collect and be prepared to tell why they think someone would collect these objects.

Instructional Strategy 2: Objects, Spaces, and George Orwell's *1984*

Read George Orwell's book *1984*. Among other things, the notion of "history" is an important feature within this book. Also, many objects rise to the surface throughout the book, such as a writing tablet, a paperweight, a picture of St. Clement Danes, and chocolate (to name just a few). Some of these objects are prominent within the book; others seem more obscure. Select an object, related group of objects, or specific space that comes into play within the pages of this book. Discuss the importance of the object(s)/space you have identified in helping us better understand the triadic relationship that exists among people, objects, and history. In other words, what significant insights are we able to draw about people and society in *1984*, and their views of history in particular, from Orwell's inclusion and discussion of this specific object, group of objects, or this space? What may we learn about our lives today from considering this view of people, objects, and history projected by Orwell in this book?

Instructional Strategy 3: A Game: Scrap This Assignment

This instructional game is designed to take place in an art museum. Students are to imagine that representatives of a clandestine group called the Supreme & Categorically Real Art Police (SCRAP) recently paid a visit to their museum. The purpose of visiting this museum was for SCRAP to identify objects housed in the museum that are not considered to be *real art* and worthy of exhibition in a fine art museum. A letter, sent to the art museum by SCRAP, identifies specific objects now on display at the museum, which this organization believes should be questioned and removed from their placement in the *art* museum (for this activity, the teacher or leader of this activity identifies these objects ahead of time). A group of three or four students is assigned to each object in the museum that SCRAP has identified as questionable. The task of each group is to study the museum-based object assigned to them, and build a case that would support or challenge the recommendations of SCRAP. Each group then has a specifically allotted time to present and discuss its case with the other group members.

Instructional Strategy 4: Identifying Important Objects and Human-Made Structures and Spaces

This learning activity is directed toward students generating discussion about objects, structures, and spaces found throughout the world. Students are divided into two groups. One group discusses the following questions: If you could collect in one place the 10 most important specific human-made objects found in the universe, what would they be? And why do you think they deserve to be on your list? For this exercise, members of this group are to exclude human-made structures and spaces from their list. The other group of students discusses the following questions: If you could visit the 10 most important structures or human formed spaces on the planet, where would you go? And why? After bringing the students back together, each group shares and discusses its lists with the entire class, along with responses to the final question, which is the same for both groups: What do you think is the single most important invention in the world since 1900? And why do you think this is so?

Instructional Strategy 5: Evolutionary Change in the Design of an Object

The design of many objects in our world, such as automobiles, irons, lawn mowers, clocks, and washing machines, has undergone significant change throughout the years. A useful exercise is to have students select a specific type of object that has undergone evolutionary alteration over time. Ask students to document this modification of design over a period of years, recording why these various changes in form may have occurred. Students are then asked to anticipate and draw, paint, or even sculpt what they believe the design of this object-type will be in 10, 50, or 100 years, and speculate why this artifact will be changed and shaped into this new form.

Instructional Strategy 6: Orientation to Fieldwork

Students can be taught how to do fieldwork by investigating local and familiar material culture. An example of this approach, developed by

Doug Blandy and John Fenn, was associated with *Public Culture and Heritage: A Beijing Based Field School*. Undergraduate and graduate students in their field school studied and documented local culture as it manifested in language, the arts, food, behaviors, beliefs, institutions, and interpersonal communication.

For conducting fieldwork in China, Doug and John asked their U.S. and Chinese students to reflect upon their own cultural setting. Because much of their work in China paired oral narratives with images, students were asked to consider how they and their family represented themselves in stories and photographs. Students were also asked to consider food within their family. This first fieldwork associated with the field school was as follows (this structure can be generalized to other types of fieldwork that students could do in relation to material culture):

Part 1. Please describe the following:

- How does your family remember people, places, and events?
- What are some of the objects in your home that have stories connected to them?
- Does your family use photos or video to remember?
- What is the oldest photo or video your family has?
- Who takes photos or video in your family?
- Who takes care of the photos or videos?
- Where are the photos or video kept?
- When does your family look at photos or video?

Part 2. Talk with a family member about a particular photograph or video:

- What stories are represented by the photo or video?
- How does this photo or video represent the values, attitudes, and beliefs of your family?
- What symbols appear in the photograph or video that represent your family's culture?

Part 3. Food is another way that a family's culture is represented:

- What distinctive foods did your parents, grandparents, or other forebears eat?
- Identify a favorite family recipe and write about why you chose it.
- Write a detailed account of what happens in your kitchen while food is being prepared.

- What makes a good meal? How should it be served? Who should be there? Who cooks, sets the table, serves, entertains, and does dishes?

Part 4. Doug and John's field school required students to create video documentaries associated with their fieldwork in China. This fourth component asked students to develop a "treatment," as if they would do a video documentary based on the material culture collected through Parts 1–3 above:

- What story does the documentary tell?
- Who are the characters in the documentary?
- What activities would you show?
- Whom would you interview on camera?
- Would there be narration, and if so, what would be narrated?
- Would you include music, and if so, what type?
- Would you include photographs or historic film or video?

Instructional Strategy 7: Imagine the Material Culture of the Future

The purposes and functions of objects change over time and context. In addition, as technology changes and as new forms of technology emerge, the ways in which the future is conceptualized may change. Futurists, based on trends that they see emerging now, imagine how those trends may manifest many years from now within possible scenarios such as those discussed below. This strategy asks students, keeping in mind their grade level, to imagine the material culture of the future.

Step 1: The Scenario. Describe a future scenario associated with everyday life. The scenario should occur at least 20 years in the future. Scenarios could be associated with schools, entertainment, travel, home, and sporting events, among others.

- Describe possible participants in the scenario.
- What are the current central concerns and key issues that are influencing the creation of material culture in this scenario?
- Describe the material culture associated with this scenario.

Step 2: Driving Forces and Trends

- What are the immediate driving forces that are likely to have the most important influence on the issues and concerns associated with the material culture in the scenario described above?

Step 3: Background

- What are the main themes or assumptions around which your scenario is built (that is, access, education, technology, economics, politics, culture, etc.)?

Instructional Strategy 8: Who Made That?

For a period of time beginning on March 7, 2011, *The New York Times Sunday Magazine* published a regular column titled "Who Made That?" Each week, an example of material culture was chosen as a focus. Examples include the kickstand, the dial tone, kale, blue jeans, the catcher's mask, the stiletto high heel, marshmallows, and the fly swatter, among many others.

"Who Made That?" can be used as a strategy for encouraging students to choose an object to investigate. A "Who Made That?" column will typically respond to several of the following questions:

- What is the object made of?
- How is the object made?
- Who invented the object? What do we know about that person or persons?
- When and where did the object originate?
- What did it first look like?
- How has the object varied across time and place?
- How did the object get its name?
- What motivated the creation of the object?
- Are there famous people or events associated with the object?
- Has the object influenced history?
- Is the object considered a collectible?
- Has the economic value of the object changed over time?
- What effect has the object had on the industry that is associated with it?
- Is the object associated with a particular gender, class, race, or ethnicity?

Instructional Strategy 9: Personal Ethnography

The study of one's self can be instructive in understanding and appreciating the material culture associated with one's personal, familial, and community life. Studying one's self, using an ethnographic approach, reveals and clarifies one's values, attitudes, and beliefs as well as those of others. Such study also illuminates the importance of material culture in everyday life. Questions like the following can guide this self-study:

- What were the core beliefs and values of your family and how were they communicated/sustained through material culture?
- What are the core beliefs and values of your immediate community now? How are they expressed through material culture?
- Are there any specific values you hold that are supported and expressed by the material culture you collect and/or create?

Instructional Strategy 10: Material Culture and Personal Customization

People express their values through the material culture associated with body ornamentation and how we clothe ourselves. For 7 days, make time each day to observe the people around you and make notes and drawings on what they are wearing as well as any ornamentation. Choose a different location for each day. Do not look for just the "outrageous." Discover both the extreme and subtle ways people choose to present themselves to the public. Interpret what it is that you believe they are saying/expressing through their personal appearance. Is there a relationship between the place where you are observing people and how people are choosing to express themselves through clothing and ornamentation?

TEN APPROACHES TO MATERIAL CULTURE STUDY

The following are 10 specific approaches to the study of material culture, drawn from writers in a variety of fields of study, which educators and learners may use for exploring objects and the value these things hold in our lives.

Approach 1: Object, Context, and Process

Margaret Stott (1987), an anthropologist and educator in British Columbia, has utilized a three-stage strategy for analyzing material culture, in which she advocates that teachers can further enhance learners' understanding of an object through establishing situations where students encounter material culture through a variety of sensory engagements. Stott calls on teachers to create instructional situations in which objects are handled by students, rather than only viewed by them. Discussing her purpose and approach to object-based teaching, Stott (1987) writes:

> My objective in teaching about material culture is to lead the student to comprehend a wide range of *kinds* of information as well as to understand specific details. There seem to me to be three different but important

dimensions to that learning experience, no matter what the level of student and no matter what the artifact being considered . . .
1. the object itself;
2. the context of the object; and
3. the process of the object's manufacture and use. (p. 14)

Through exercises that include comparing and contrasting objects, initiating questions about specific objects, and proposing adjectives that reflect an individual's emotional response to these objects, Stott engages her students in various processes of material culture study. For Stott, the exploration of material culture is not only an investigation of artifacts from other times and places, but also involves the examination of contemporary and nearby objects and their meanings within our world today.

Approach 2: Description, Classification, and Interpretation

Craig Gilborn, writing for *Museum News* in 1968, stated, "Objects are capable of yielding a considerable amount of information about themselves and the conditions in which they were formed or fashioned" (p. 13). Delving into this notion, Gilborn has formed a three-part system for investigating material culture, particularly well-known types of objects that undergo modification over time, yet still retain their primary recognizable features. The object Gilborn uses to exemplify his investigative approach is the Coca-Cola bottle. Exploring the meaning of this cultural artifact, Gilborn believes the investigation of an object is a multifaceted engagement, consisting of three operations—description, classification, and interpretation:

1. Descriptive Operation. Describe the object in terms of shape, details, materials, color, weight, and so forth. Gilborn (1968) suggests, when possible, that students have direct contact with the objects studied, leading to "*an awareness of the diverse attributional character of objects*" (p. 14).
2. Classification Operation. Classification is accomplished, according to Gilborn (1968), based on comparisons made with other similar objects, in which "differences in attributes can be explained in terms of changed behavior or altered conditions, usually as they have taken place over a period of years" (p. 14).
3. Interpretive Operation. Gilborn (1968) completes the three-step operational process with interpretation: "Interpretation is the culminating objective since it addresses itself to the broad question, *What possible meanings can be derived from the*

products of our labors" (p. 16)? In other words, what meaning can be drawn from our investigation of this object?

The study of material culture is a search for meaning in and through objects. Gilborn's three-operation approach to the exploration of objects—in this case, the ubiquitous Coca-Cola bottle—offers teachers and students a worthwhile strategy to consider when investigating items of material culture.

Approach 3: Investigating Handcrafted Objects

Michael Owen Jones, professor of folklore and history at UCLA, looks particularly at handcrafted objects. Specifically, Jones (1993) has studied handmade wooden chairs, "to examine the making of each chair as a unique occurrence" (p. 193). For Jones, the touching and handling of objects is crucial to an understanding of how and why these objects were made. Jones (1993) has proposed this four-part strategy for investigating material culture:

1. Technology. The tools, techniques of construction, and materials as well as the ends to which the object is to be put and the means for achieving these objectives.
2. Producer. The craftsperson's self-concept, motivations, and aspirations; knowledge of and skill at this endeavor; values; and intentions and criteria of formal excellence in addition to preferences and predilections on the basis of which a characteristic mode of execution, construction, and presentation develops.
3. Consumer. Customer stipulation of form, materials, and design elements as well as selection and treatment of and comments about the object or objects from which the craftsperson is likely to infer values, attitudes, preferences, and associations that inform expectations, satisfaction, and uses or functions.
4. Product-Producer Interface. Models and precedents for a work, the requirements of useful design (for example, appearance, access, strength, and durability), the process of conceptualization as it affects and is affected by implementation and the craft identity, activity, or product as a vehicle of expression or locus of symbols. (pp. 193–194)

Although Jones has focused his attention on the study of handmade chairs, this four-part approach to the investigation of objects has application for exploring a wide range of material culture, particularly those constructions made by hand.

Approach 4: Five Properties and Four Operations of Object Study

This approach to artifact study proposed by E. McClung Fleming (1974) consists of a five-part system of classifying the basic features of an object, and subsequently four operations played out on these five properties. According to Fleming, the five properties of a human-made object are its history, material, construction, design, and function:

> History. Where and when the object was made, by whom and for whom, and why successive changes in ownership, condition, and function occurred.
> Material. What the object is made of—wood, fibers, ceramic bodies, metals, glass, and so on.
> Construction. Techniques of manufacture, workmanship, and the way parts are organized to bring about the object's function.
> Design. The structure, form, style, ornament, and iconography of the object.
> Function. Both the uses (intended functions) and the roles (unintended functions) of the object in its culture, including utility, delight, and communication. (p. 166)

After his discussion of the five basic properties, Fleming (1974) then shifts to the operational phase of his object investigation. He offers the four operations of identification, evaluation, cultural analysis, and interpretation that, when performed on the five properties, help us gain essential information about the object in question. A concise explanation of each operation follows:

> Identification (classification, authentication, description). This results in a body of distinctive facts about the artifact.
> Evaluation. The evaluative assessment of an object initiates a set of judgments about the artifact, usually based on comparisons with other examples of its kind.
> Cultural Analysis. This examines the various interrelationships of an artifact and its contemporary culture.
> Interpretation. This suggests the meaning and significance of the artifact in relation to aspects of our own culture. (p. 167–173)

Fleming's (1974) model for object analysis provides a multidimensional format for exploring the many facets of an object, leading to greater understanding of the meaning and significance of material culture in the past and for the world today.

Approach 5: 14 Points of Access for Studying an Object

Charles F. Montgomery proposes 14 points of possible access that provide avenues for the investigation of an object. Montgomery's (1982) entry sites for examining an object are as follows:

1. Overall Appearance. Examine and encounter the object from various angles. How do I react to it?
2. Form. In handling the object, record measurements, weights, proportions, plus evidence of any repairs or alterations.
3. Ornament. For any ornamentation ask: Why is it there? Does it appear to accomplish its purpose? Is the overall affect the better for its presence?
4. Color. Does the color appear to be original or has it been changed over time?
5. Analysis of Materials. Gather and assess information on the individual materials (for example, wood, metal, fabric, plastic). Use instruments such as a magnifying glass, camera, or microscope.
6. Techniques Employed by the Craftsman [Craftsperson]. Examine the object to determine the construction techniques used by the maker.
7. Trade Practices. Do any brand names, symbols, or identifying marks exist on the object? Do they help give a location of its origin?
8. Function. Why was the object made? What was the intent of the maker? Can the object have adequately performed the uses for which it was intended?
9. Style. Does the object appear to display characteristics of a certain period or broad movement in art, technology, or society?
10. Date. The object's appearance, form, and ornament can help date it. Also look for any stamp, signature, or actual date mark.
11. Attribution. Is there a maker's signature or mark? Identification may also be made by the particular style of the object.
12. History of the Object and Its Ownership. Is there any documentation of the object through sales records, exhibition catalogs, or family histories?
13. Condition. Is there evidence of natural aging and wear, such as discoloration, softening of edges, corners, and contours? Have repairs been made?
14. Appraisal or Evaluation. By what criteria will this object be appraised or valued—monetarily, historical significance, religious meaning, and so on?

Each of Montgomery's (1982) 14 exploratory steps may not be applicable in the investigation of every object. Yet, this comprehensive list provides an engaging series of entry points to consider in helping initiate and carry out systematic and meaningful examination of the material culture that surrounds us.

Approach 6: A Multisensory Approach to Object Study

In his book chapter "Visual Aesthetics for Five Senses and Four Dimensions: An Ethnographic Approach to Aesthetic Objects," John Forrest (1991) uses a traditional quilt as his object of study. Forrest's proposal for object analysis is based on employing, when possible, a full range of sensory engagements. Advocating that touch, hearing, taste, smell, and sight all be utilized (or at least considered for use) in the investigation of an object, Forrest believes that his conversation about the sensory analysis of material culture provides an opportunity for the deep and rich exploration of a wide range of objects.

Beyond utilizing the five senses to explore objects, Forrest (1991) urges that material culture be considered in multidimensional ways, through the contexts of height, width, depth, and time. How is a specific object constructed in three dimensions, and how does time affect both its substance (for example, fading, wear, breakage), as well as the manner in which it is viewed (for instance, by way of natural light at certain times of the day or seasons of the year)? Utilizing his example object, Forrest (1991) writes:

> Quilts live in rooms with windows where light quality and direction change hour by hour, day by day, and month by month. Dramatically different light qualities radically change colors and shades.... Quilters lovingly run their hands across a quilt softened with many washings, and sometimes differential fading and bleeding of dyes produce dramatic results. (p. 53)

Through the employment of all our senses, and not only sight, Forrest calls for an expanded approach to the study of objects, one in which we explore objects in new and creative ways as we engage in multidimensional and multisensory investigations of the material culture that makes up our world.

Forrest's approach is particularly significant because it responds to the multisensory lifestyles that extend far beyond the visual and shape our daily lives as we participate in increasingly more sophisticated and sensory-filled multimedia environments.

Conclusion

Approach 7: Collaborative Ethnography

Luke Lassiter's (2004) method of working with members of communities and cultures to responsively discover the unique features and characteristics of those communities and cultures is referred to as collaborative ethnography. Lassiter promotes this method as one way to try to achieve a correct interpretation, representation, or description of a cultural group and the material culture it produces, uses, collects, or preserves.

Lassiter's (2004) method includes the following:

1. Participating in the lives of others (which may include learning a new language or learning how to behave appropriately within a particular setting);
2. Observing behavior (which may include that of the ethnographer herself as well as that of the community);
3. Taking field notes (which may include jotting down first impressions, drawing maps, or writing extensive descriptions of cultural scenes); and
4. Conducting interviews (which may include both informal conversations and more formal exchanges). (p. 2)

This approach is educationally valuable because it is easily applied and can be adapted for use across educational levels. It can be effectively applied to the study of one's own family or community as well as communities that are less familiar. One of the strengths of this approach is the relationships that are fostered through the use of the method as well as the opportunity to confirm insights with members of the community or culture.

Approach 8: Mapping

Mapping is one way that people reflect on and communicate about environments that surround them. Mapping can be used to encourage representations of multisensory environments and the material culture that forms them, as in the multisensory maps collected by Katherine Harmon (2003), and by Janet Abrams and Peter Hall (2006). Both these publications present extraordinary examples of maps that chart computer networks, conversations between people, smells within a transportation system, three-dimensional subway schemes, navigation by vegetation, stress levels in neighborhoods, pleasure and pain, dreams, and imaginary places, among many others.

For example, a mapping project begins by asking students to map an unfamiliar human-made interior or exterior environment using a multisensory approach. Students are called on to center their attention toward the built environment and the traces (material culture) of human activity that occur within it. Students are asked to create a multilayered map that focuses on at least three of the five senses. Students begin the mapping process by spending at least 1 hour in their chosen location. Fieldnotes and drawings that record their sensory experience at the site are used later to create at least three maps using 8½-by-11-inch transparent acetate sheets, one map for each of their chosen senses. Each map is completed in a different color and to the same scale. In this way, the maps can be overlaid to provide a representation of their multisensory experience in the space.

Approach 9: A Five-Step Approach for Exploring Objects

Jules David Prown is a professor emeritus of art history at Yale University, where he taught for almost 40 years. Throughout this time, he instructed a longstanding course in material culture for art history students, and through it developed a process of object investigation and analysis utilizing five successive steps that he and his students have used quite successfully. Prown is earnestly deliberate in his approach to the study of objects, yet he does not intend for his five-step approach to be viewed as unreasonably constrictive in its structure. Rather, Prown has established this rigid framework of sequential analytic process to be followed in a strict order because he believes such activity "prolongs the information gathering process and defers the judgmental process as much as possible" (Prown & Haltman, 2000, p. xii). This five-step process for investigating material culture is described through the words of Prown and Kenneth Haltman (2000):

1. Description. "Thoroughly describe this object, paying careful attention, as relevant, to all of its aspects—material, spatial, and temporal. Be attentive to details . . . but ever keep an eye on the big picture" (p. 3).
2. Deduction. "Elucidate your intellectual and sensory responses to your chosen object in the form of deductions, drawing insight and evidence from your own previous description." When complete, "Now elucidate your emotional responses in similar fashion, again drawing insight and evidence from your own previous description" (p. 5).
3. Speculation. "It is now possible to entertain hypotheses concerning what your chosen object signifies, what is suggests about the world in which it circulates or circulated—a world which, in some sense . . . it represents" (p. 6).

4. Research. "Think creatively about what research would be necessary to test your interpretive hypotheses, detailing whatever speculations you find yourself entertaining, anticipating the argument you can imagine yourself eventually making, and prepare a plan of action . . . accompanied by an annotated bibliography" (p. 6).
5. Interpretive Analysis. Your interpretive analysis "should digest, develop, and present perceptions generated from these [previous four] exercises, but differ from them in being structured by an *argument*, a clearly worded *claim* defended through detailed references to both the object . . . and its context" (p. 7).

Approach 10: A Framework of Ideas and Questions for Analyzing Objects

A wonderfully practical resource that anyone wanting to study material culture should read is Gail Durbin, Susan Morris, and Sue Wilkinson's *A Teacher's Guide to Learning from Objects* (1990). This concise handbook can be used with learners of all ages and is filled with exemplary information and instructional examples for helping explorations of objects come alive for students. Among a fabulous array of learning activity ideas and motivations for investigating material culture, the book offers a very useful framework of ideas and questions for analyzing objects, which is presented here. Readers are encouraged to examine Durbin, Morris, and Wilkinson's publication to secure excellent extension questions and a plethora of rich ideas for investigating objects.

Investigating an Object

Durbin, Morris, and Wilkinson (1990) encourage educators to ask questions about objects in the following way:

- Physical Features (What does it look and feel like?)
- Construction (How was it made?)
- Function (What was it made for?)
- Design (Is it well designed?)
- Value (What is it worth?)

How Do We Find Out?

- Observation
- Research/Knowledge
- Discussion

Selected Books Relating to Material Culture, with Interest Toward Art Education

Abraham, D. S. (2015). *The elements of power: Gadgets, guns, and the struggle for sustainable future in the rare metal age.* New Haven, CT: Yale University Press.

Adshead, S. A. M. (1997). *Material culture in Europe and China, 1400–1800: The rise of consumerism.* New York, NY: St. Martin's Press.

Ago, R. (2013). *Gusto for things: A history of objects in seventeenth-century Rome.* Chicago, IL: University of Chicago Press.

Andrews, D. C. (2015). *Shopping: Material culture perspectives.* Newark, DE: University of Delaware Press.

Appadurai, A. (Ed.). (1988). *The social life of things: Commodities in cultural perspective.* Cambridge, UK: University of Cambridge.

Aram, B., & Yun-Casalilla, B. (Eds.). (2014). *Global goods and the Spanish empire, 1492–1824: Circulation, resistance and diversity.* London, UK: Palgrave Macmillan.

Arnoldi, M. J. (Ed.). (2016). *Engaging Smithsonian objects through science, history, and the arts.* Washington, DC: Smithsonian Institution Scholarly Press.

Arnoldi, M. J., Geary, C. M., & Hardin, K. L. (Eds.). (1996). *African material culture.* Bloomington, IN: Indiana University Press.

Attfield, J. (2000). *Wild things: The material culture of everyday life.* New York, NY: Berg.

Barringer, T., & Flynn, T. (Eds.). (1998). *Colonialism and the object: Empire, material culture and the museum.* London, UK: Routledge.

Baudrillard, J. (2006). *The system of objects.* London, UK: Verso.

Bauer, A. J. (2001). *Goods, power, history: Latin America's material culture.* Cambridge, UK: Cambridge University Press.

Beaudry, M. C. (2006). *Findings: The material culture of needlework and sewing.* New Haven, CT: Yale University Press.

Bennett, J. (2010). *Vibrant matter: A political ecology of things.* Durham, NC: Duke University Press.

Berger, A. A. (1992). *Reading matter: Multidisciplinary perspectives on material culture*. New Brunswick, NJ: Transaction Publishers.

Berger, A. A. (2014). *What objects mean: An introduction to material culture* (2nd ed.). New York, NY: Routledge.

Betsky, A. (Ed.). (1997). *Icons: Magnets of meaning*. San Francisco, CA: San Francisco Museum of Modern Art.

Bogost, I. (2016). *Play anything: The pleasure of limits, the uses of boredom, and the secret of games*. New York, NY: Basic Books.

Boivin, N. (2008). *Material cultures, material minds: The impact of things on human thought, society, and evolution*. New York, NY: Cambridge University Press.

Bolin, P. E., & Blandy, D. (Eds.). (2011). *Matter matters: Art education and material culture studies*. Reston, VA: National Art Education Association.

Bolin, P. E., Blandy, D., & Congdon, K. G. (Eds.). (2000). *Remembering others: Making invisible histories of art education visible*. Reston, VA: National Art Education Association.

Bormann, F. H., Balmori, D., & Geballe, G. T. (2001). *Redesigning the American lawn: A search for environmental harmony* (2nd ed.). New Haven, CT: Yale University Press.

Bronner, S. J. (Ed.). (1986). *Grasping things: Folk material culture and mass society in America*. Lexington, KY: University Press of Kentucky.

Brown, D. E. (2002). *Inventing modern America: From the microwave to the mouse*. Cambridge, MA: MIT Press.

Browne, R. B., & Browne, P. (1991). *Digging into popular culture: Theories and methodologies in archeology, anthropology and other fields*. Bowling Green, OH: Bowling Green State University Popular Press.

Browne, R. B., & Fishwick, M. (1978). *Icons of America*. Bowling Green, OH: Bowling Green State University Popular Press.

Buchli, V. (Ed.). (2002). *The material culture reader*. Oxford, UK: Berg.

Card, J. J. (Ed.). (2013). *The archaeology of hybrid material culture*. Carbondale, IL: Southern Illinois University Press.

Cardwell, D. (2001). *Wheels, clocks, and rockets: A history of technology*. New York, NY: W. W. Norton.

Certeau, M. D. (1984). *The practice of everyday life*. Berkeley, CA: University of California Press.

Chatterjee, H. J., & Hannan, L. (2016). *Engaging the senses: Object-based learning in higher education*. New York, NY: Routledge.

Chilton, E. S. (Ed.). (1999). *Material meanings: Critical approaches to the interpretation of material culture*. Salt Lake City, UT: University of Utah Press.

Chumley, L. (2016). *Creativity class: Art school and culture work in postcolonialist China*. Princeton, NJ: Princeton University Press.

Clarke, A. J. (1999). *Tupperware: The promise of plastic in 1950s America*. Washington, DC: Smithsonian.

Classen, C. (1998). *The color of angels: Cosmology, gender and the aesthetic*. New York, NY: Routledge.

Classen, C. (2012). *The deepest sense: A cultural history of touch*. Urbana, IL: University of Illinois Press.

Classen, C., Howes, D., & Synnott, A. (1994). *Aroma: The cultural history of smell*. New York, NY: Routledge.

Clifford, J. (1988). *The predicament of culture: Twentieth-century ethnography*. Cambridge, MA: Harvard University Press.

Clunas, C. (2004). *Superfluous things: Material culture and social status in early modern China*. Honolulu, HI: University of Hawaii Press.

Cohen, L. H. (1997). *Glass, paper, beans: Revelations on the nature and value of ordinary things*. New York, NY: Doubleday.

Congdon, K. G., Blandy, D., & Bolin, P. E. (Eds.). (2001). *Histories of community-based art education*. Reston, VA: National Art Education Association.

Conn, S. (2010). *Do museums still need objects?* Philadelphia, PA: University of Pennsylvania Press.

Corbin, A. (2000). *Material culture of steamboat passengers: Archaeological evidence from the Missouri River*. New York, NY: Kluwer Academic/Plenum Publishers.

Craciun, A., & Schaffer, S. (Eds.). (2016). *Palgrave studies in the Enlightenment, Romanticism and cultures of print: The material cultures of enlightenment arts and sciences*. London, UK: Springer Nature.

Csikszentmihalyi, M., & Rochberg-Halton, E. (1981). *The meaning of things: Domestic symbols and the self*. Cambridge, UK: Cambridge University Press.

Cummings, N., & Lewandowska, M. (2000). *The value of things*. Basel, Switzerland: Birkhauser.

D'Aluisio, F., & Menzel, P. (1998). *Women in the material world*. San Francisco, CA: Sierra Club Books.

Daniels, I. (2010). *The Japanese house: Material culture in the modern home (Materializing culture)*. Oxford, UK: Berg.

Dant, T. (1999). *Material culture in the social world: Values, activities, lifestyles*. Buckingham, UK: Open University Press.

Daston, L. (Ed.). (2004). *Things that talk*. Boston, MA: Zone Books.

De Cunzo, L. A., & Herman, B. L. (Eds.). (1996). *Historical archaeology and the study of American culture*. Winterthur, DE: The Henry Francis du Pont Winterthur Museum, Inc.

Deetz, J. (1996). *In small things forgotten: The archaeology of early American life* (Rev. ed.). Garden City, NY: Anchor Books.

Derevenski, J. S. (2000). *Children and material culture*. New York, NY: Routledge.

Dormer, P. (Ed.). (1997). *The culture of craft*. Manchester, UK: Manchester University Press.

Douglas, M., & Isherwood, B. (1996). *The world of goods: Toward and anthropology of consumption*. London, UK: Routledge.

Drazin, A., & Küchler, S. (2015). *The social life of materials: Studies in materials and society*. London, UK: Bloomsbury.

Durbin, G., Morris, S., & Wilkinson, S. (1990). *A teacher's guide to learning from objects*. London, UK: English Heritage.

Edgar, A., & Sedgwick, P. (Eds.). (2008). *Cultural theory: Key concepts* (2nd ed.). New York, NY: Routledge.

Edwards, E., & Hart, J. (Eds.). (2004). *Photographs objects histories: On the materiality of images*. New York, NY: Routledge.

Edwards, E., Phillips, R., & Gosden, C. (Eds.). (2006). *Sensible objects: Colonialism, museums and material culture*. Oxford, UK: Berg Publishers.

Elsner, J., & Cardinal, R. (Eds.). (1994). *The cultures of collecting*. Cambridge, MA: Harvard.

Ezell, M. J. M., & O'Keeffe, K. O. (Eds.). (1994). *Cultural artifacts and the production of meaning: The page, image, and the body*. Ann Arbor, MI: University of Michigan Press.

Fariello, A. M., & Owen, P. (Ed.). (2005). *Objects and meaning: New perspectives on art and craft*. Lanham, MD: Scarecrow Press.

Ferguson, L. (Ed.). (1977). *Historical archaeology and the importance of material things*. Charleston, SC: The Society for Historical Archaeology.

Findlen, P. (Ed.). (2013). *Early modern things: Objects and their histories, 1500–1800*. London, UK: Routledge.

Forty, A. (1986). *Objects of desire: Design and society since 1750*. London, UK: Thames & Hudson.

Francis-Jones, R., & Frampton, K. (2013). *Architecture as material culture: The work of Francis-Jones Morehen Thorp*. New York, NY: ORO Editions.

Frost, R. O., & Steketee, G. (2010). *Stuff: Compulsive hoarding and the meaning of things*. Boston, MA: Houghton Mifflin Harcourt.

Galison, P. L. (1997). *Image and logic: A material culture of microphysics*. Chicago, IL: University of Illinois Press.

Gerritsen, A., & Riello G. (Eds.). (2015). *Writing material culture history*. London, UK: Bloomsbury.

Gerritsen, A., & Riello G. (Eds.). (2016). *The global lives of things: The material culture of connections in the early modern world*. London, UK: Routledge.

Gilchrist, R. (1993). *Gender and material culture: The archaeology of religious women*. New York, NY: Routledge.

Glassie, H. H. (1999a). *Material culture*. Bloomington, IN: Indiana University Press.

Glassie, H. H. (1999b). *The potter's art*. Bloomington, IN: Indiana University Press.

Glassie, H. H. (2000). *Vernacular architecture*. Bloomington, IN: Indiana University Press.

Glenn, J., & Hayes, C. (2007). *Taking things seriously: 75 objects with unexpected significance*. New York, NY: Princeton Architectural Press.

Gosden, C., & Knowles, C. (2001). *Collecting colonialism: Material culture and colonial change*. Oxford, UK: Berg Publishing.

Gottdiener, M. (1995). *Postmodern semiotics: Material culture and the forms of postmodern life.* Oxford, UK: B. Blackwell.

Gould, R. A., & Schiffer, M. B. (Eds.). (1981). *Modern material culture: The archaeology of us.* New York, NY: Academic Press.

Graham, J. S. (1989). *Hispanic-American material culture: An annotated directory of collections, sites, archives, and festivals in the United States.* New York, NY: Greenwood Press.

Guilfoil, J. K., & Sandler, A. R. (Eds.). (1999). *Built environment education in art education.* Reston, VA: National Art Education Association.

Gunn, F. (1973). *The artificial face: A history of cosmetics.* New York, NY: Hippocrene.

Hafertepe, K. (2016). *The material culture of German Texans.* College Station, TX: Texas A&M University Press.

Hallam, E., Hockey, J., & Miller, D. (2002). *Death, memory and material culture.* New York, NY: New York University Press.

Hanley, S. B. (1999). *Everyday things in pre-modern Japan: The hidden legacy of material culture.* London, UK: University of California Press.

Harvey, K. (Ed.). (2009). *History and material culture: A student's guide to approaching alternative sources.* London, UK: Routledge.

Helland, J., Lemire, B., & Buis, A. (Eds.). (2014). *Craft, community and the material culture of place and politics, 19th and 20th century.* Burlington, VT: Ashgate.

Henare, A., Holbraad, M., & Wastell, S. (Eds.). (2007). *Thinking through things: Theorising artefacts ethnographically.* New York, NY: Routledge.

Heneghan, B. T. (2003). *Whitewashing America: Material culture and race in the antebellum imagination.* Jackson, MS: University Press of Mississippi.

Hicks, D., & Beaudry, M. C. (Eds.). (2010). *Oxford handbook of material culture studies.* New York, NY: Oxford University Press.

Hindle, B. (Ed.). (1981). *Material culture of the wooden age.* Tarrytown, NY: Sleepy Hollow Press.

Hodder, I. (Ed.). (1989). *The meaning of things: Material culture and symbolic expression.* London, UK: Unwin Hyman.

Hodder, I. (Ed.). (1991). *Archaeological theory in Europe: The last three decades.* London, UK: Routledge.

Hodder, I. (Ed.). (1995). *Interpreting archaeology: Finding meaning in the past.* London, UK: Routledge.

Hodder, I., & Hutson, S. (2003). *Reading the past: Current approaches to interpretation in archaeology* (3rd ed.). Cambridge, UK: Cambridge University Press.

Hooker, R. J. (1981). *Food and drink in America: A history.* Indianapolis, IN: Bobbs-Merrill.

Howes, D., & Classen, C. (2014). *Ways of sensing: Understanding the senses in society.* New York, NY: Routledge.

Hudson, T., & Blackburn, T. C. (1982). *Material culture of the Chumash interaction sphere*. Los Altos, CA: Ballena Press; Santa Barbara, CA: Santa Barbara Museum of Natural History.

Hugill, P. J., & Dickson, D. B. (Eds.). (1988). *The transfer and transformation of ideas and material culture*. College Station, TX: Texas A & M University Press.

Hume, D. L. (2014). *Tourism art and souvenirs: The material culture of tourism*. London, UK: Routledge.

Humes, E. (2013). *Garbology: Our dirty love affair with trash*. New York, NY: Penguin Group.

Ingersoll, Jr., D. W., & Bronitsky, G. (Eds.). (1987). *Mirror and metaphor: Material and social constructions of reality*. Lanham, MD: University Press of America.

Jackson, J. B. (1984). *Discovering the vernacular landscape*. New Haven, CT: Yale University Press.

Jackson, J. B. (1994). *A sense of place, a sense of time*. New Haven, CT: Yale University Press.

Jaffee, D. (2010). *A new nation of goods: The material culture of early America*. Philadelphia, PA: University of Pennsylvania Press.

Jenkins, V. S. (1994). *The lawn: A history of an American obsession*. Washington, DC: Smithsonian Institution Press.

Jones, A. (2007). *Memory and material culture*. New York, NY: Cambridge University Press.

Jones, C. (Ed.). (2006). *Sensorium: Embodied experience, technology, and contemporary art*. Cambridge, MA: MIT.

Kammen, M. (1999). *American culture, American tastes: Social change and the 20th century*. New York, NY: Knopf.

Kingery, W. D. (Ed.). (1996). *Learning from things: Method and theory of material culture studies*. Washington, DC: Smithsonian Institution Press.

Knappett, C. (2005). *Thinking through material culture: An interdisciplinary perspective*. Philadelphia, PA: University of Pennsylvania Press.

Koch, G. (1983). *Material culture of Tuvalu*. Suva, Fiji: University of the South Pacific.

Kolsbun, K. (2008). *Peace: The biography of a symbol*. Washington, DC: National Geographic Society.

Koltun-Fromm, K. (2010). *Material culture and Jewish thought in America*. Bloomington, IN: Indiana University Press.

Korn, P. (2013). *Why we make things and why it matters: The education of a craftsman*. Boston, MA: David R. Godine.

Kubler, G. (1962). *The shape of time: Remarks on the history of things*. New Haven, CT: Yale University Press.

Kuchler, S., & Miller, D. (2005). *Clothing as material culture*. Thousand Oaks, CA: Sage Publications.

Kyvig, D. E., & Marty, M. A. (2010). *Nearby history: Exploring the past around you* (3rd. ed.). Walnut Creek, CA: AltaMira Press.

Lemonnier, P. (Ed.). (1993). *Technological choices: Transformation in material culture since the Neolithic.* London, UK: Routledge.

Levent, N., & Pascual-Leone, A. (Eds.). (2014). *The multisensory museum: Cross-disciplinary perspectives on touch, sound, smell, memory, and space.* Lanham, MD: Rowman & Littlefield.

Levy, J. (2002). *Really useful: The origins of everyday things.* Willowdale, Canada: Firefly.

Lubar, S., & Kendrick, K. M. (2001). *Legacies: Collecting America's history at the Smithsonian.* Washington, DC: Smithsonian Institution Press.

Lubar, S., & Kingery, W. D. (1993). *History from things: Essays on material culture.* Washington, DC: Smithsonian Institution Press.

Lukas, P. (1997). *Inconspicuous consumption: An obsessive look at the stuff we take for granted, from the everyday to the obscure.* New York, NY: Crown Trade Paperbacks.

MacGregor, N. (2011). *A history of the world in 100 objects.* New York, NY: Viking.

Margolies, J. (1993). *Pump and circumstance: Glory days of the gas station.* Boston, MA: Little, Brown, and Company.

Martin, A. S., & Garrison, J. R. (Eds.). (1997). *American material culture: The shape of the field.* Winterthur, DE: The Henry Francis du Pont Winterthur Museum, Inc.

Martinez, K., & Ames, K. L. (Eds.). (1997). *The material culture of gender, the gender of material culture.* Winterthur, DE: Henry Francis du Pont Winterthur Museum, Inc.

Maudlin, D., & Herman, B. L. (2016). *Building the British Atlantic world: Spaces, places, and material culture, 1600–1850.* Chapel Hill, NC: University of North Carolina Press.

Mayo, E. (1984). *American material culture: The shape of things around us.* Bowling Green, OH: Bowling Green State University Press.

McCracken, G. (1991). *Culture and consumption.* Bloomington, IN: Indiana University Press.

McDannell, C. (1995). *Material Christianity: Religion and popular culture in America.* New Haven, CT: Yale University Press.

McFee, J. K. (1970). *Preparation for art* (2nd ed.). Belmont, CA: Wadsworth.

McFee, J. K., & Degge, R. M. (1980). *Art, culture, and environment.* Dubuque, IA: Kendall/Hunt.

McLuhan, M., & McLuhan, E. (1988). *Laws of media.* Toronto, Canada: University of Toronto.

Menzel, P. (1994). *Material world: A global family portrait.* San Francisco, CA: Sierra Club Books.

Miller, D. (1987). *Material culture and mass consumption.* Oxford, UK: B. Blackwell.

Miller, D. (Ed.). (1998). *Material cultures: Why some things matter.* Chicago, IL: University of Chicago Press.

Miller, D. (Ed.). (2001a). *Car cultures.* Oxford, UK: Berg.

Miller, D. (Ed.). (2001b). *Home possessions: Material culture behind closed doors.* Oxford, UK: Berg.
Miller, D. (Ed.). (2005). *Materiality.* Durham, NC: Duke University Press
Miller, D. (2008). *The comfort of things.* Somerset, NJ: John Wiley & Sons, Inc.
Miller, D. (2010). *Stuff.* Malden, MA: Polity Press.
Miller, D., & Tilley, C. (Ed.). (1984). *Ideology, power, and prehistory.* Cambridge, UK: Cambridge University Press.
Miodownik, M. (2013). *Stuff matters: Exploring the marvelous materials that shape our man-made world.* London, UK: Penguin.
Morgan, D. (Ed.). (2009). *Religion and material culture: The matter of belief.* New York, NY: Routledge.
Motz, M. F., & Browne, P. (Eds.). (1988). *Making the American home: Middle-class women & domestic material culture 1840–1940.* Bowling Green, OH: Bowling Green State University Popular Press.
Murthy, K. K. (1983). *Material culture of Sanchi.* Delhi, India: Sundeep.
Myers, F. R. (Ed.). (2001). *The empire of things: Regimes of value and material culture.* Santa Fe, NM: School of American Research Press.
Nelson, M. J. (Ed.). (1994). *Material culture and people's art among the Norwegians in America.* Northfield, MN: Norwegian-American Historical Association.
Norman, D. A. (2004). *Emotional design: Why we love (or hate) everyday things.* New York, NY: Basic Books.
Norman, D. A. (2013). *The design of everyday things.* New York, NY: Basic Books.
Painter, C. (Ed.). (2002). *Contemporary art and the home.* Oxford, UK: Oxford University Press.
Panati, C. (1987). *Extraordinary origins of everyday things.* New York, NY: Harper & Row.
Patrick, B., & Thompson, J. (2009). *An uncommon history of common things.* Washington, DC: National Geographic Society.
Pearce, S. M. (Ed.). (1989). *Museum studies in material culture.* London, UK: Leicester University Press.
Pearce, S. M. (Ed.). (1997). *Experiencing material culture in the Western world.* London, UK: Leicester University Press.
Pearson, M. P., & Richards, C. (1994). *Architecture and order: Approaches to social space.* London, UK: Routledge.
Peck, W. H. (2013). *The material world of ancient Egypt.* New York, NY: Cambridge University Press.
Peterson, E. (2004). *Roadside Americana: Landmark tourist attractions.* Lincolnwood, IL: Publications International, Ltd.
Petroski, H. (1992). *The pencil: A history of design and circumstance.* New York, NY: Alfred A. Knopf.
Petroski, H. (1994). *The evolution of useful things: How everyday artifacts—from forks and pins to paper clips and zippers—came to be as they are.* New York, NY: Random House.

Petroski, H. (2015). *An uncommon history of common things* (Vol. 2). Washington, DC: National Geographic Society.

Plate, S. B. (2014). *A history of religion in 5½ objects*. Boston, MA: Beacon Press.

Pocius, G. L. (Ed.). (1991). *Living in a material world: Canadian and American approaches to material culture*. Saint John's, Newfoundland, Canada: Institute of Social and Economic Research.

Potvin, J., & Myzelev, A. (Eds.). (2009). *Material cultures, 1740–1920: The meanings and pleasures of collecting*. London, UK: Ashgate Publishing Company.

Pounds, N. J. (1993). *Hearth & home: A history of material culture*. Bloomington, IN: Indiana University Press.

Prown, J. D., & Haltman, K. (Eds.). (2000). *American artifacts: Essays in material culture*. East Lansing, MI: Michigan State University Press.

Quimby, I. M. G. (Ed.). (1978). *Material culture and the study of American life*. Winterthur, DE: Henry Francis du Pont Winterthur Museum, Inc.

Rathje, W., &, Murphy, C. (2001). *Rubbish!: The archaeology of garbage*. Tucson, AZ: University of Arizona Press.

Reinarz, J. (2014). *Past scents: Historical perspectives on smell*. Urbana, IL: University of Illinois Press.

Renfrew, C., & Scarre, C. (1998). *Cognition and material culture: The archaeology of symbolic storage*. Cambridge, UK: McDonald Institute for Archaeological Research.

Reynolds, B., & Stott, M. A. (Eds.). (1987). *Material anthropology: Contemporary approaches to material culture*. Lanham, MD: University Press of America.

Richardson, C., Hamling, T., & Gaimster, D. (Eds.). (2017). *The Routledge handbook of material culture in early modern Europe*. New York, NY: Routledge.

Riggins, S. H. (Ed.). (1994). *The socialness of things: Essays on the socio-semiotics of objects*. Berlin, Germany: Mouton de Gruyter.

Roe, K. E. (1988). *Corncribs in history, folklife, & architecture*. Ames, IA: Iowa State University Press.

Rogers, H. (2006). *Gone tomorrow: The hidden life of garbage*. New York, NY: The New Press.

Ronnenberg, H. W. (2011). *Material culture of breweries (Guides to historical artifacts)*. Walnut Creek, CA: Left Coast Press.

Rose, D. (2014). *Enchanted objects: Design, human desire, and the Internet of things*. New York, NY: Scribner.

Rosenzweig, R., & Thelen, D. (1998). *The presence of the past: Popular uses of history in American life*. New York, NY: Columbia University Press.

Saunders, N. (Ed.). (2004). *Matters of conflict: Material culture, memory, and the First World War*. London, UK: Routledge.

Schiffer, M. B. (1991). *The portable radio in American life*. Tucson, AZ: University of Arizona Press.

Schiffer, M. B. (1999). *The material life of human beings: Artifacts, behavior, and communication.* London, UK: Routledge.

Schlereth, T. J. (1980). *Artifacts and the American past.* Nashville, TN: American Association for State and Local History.

Schlereth, T. J. (Ed.). (1982). *Material culture studies in America.* Nashville, TN: American Association for State and Local History.

Schlereth, T. J. (Ed.). (1985). *Material culture: A research guide.* Lawrence, KS: University Press of Kansas.

Schlereth, T. J. (1992). *Cultural history & material culture: Everyday life, landscapes, and museums.* Charlottesville, VA: University Press of Virginia.

Schlereth, T. J. (1997). *Reading the road: U.S. 40 and the American landscape.* Knoxville, TN: The University of Tennessee Press.

Schroeder, F. E. H. (1993). *Front yard America: The evolution and meanings of a vernacular domestic landscape.* Bowling Green, OH: Bowling Green State University Popular Press.

Sciama, L. D., & Eicher, J. B. (Eds.). (1998). *Beads and beadmakers: Gender, material culture and meaning.* Oxford, UK: Berg.

Sennett, R. (2008). *The craftsman.* New Haven, CT: Yale University Press.

Sharma, R. S. (1983). *Material culture and social formations in ancient India.* Delhi, India: MacMillan India Limited.

Sheumaker, H., & Wajda, S. T. (Eds.). (2008). *Material culture in America: Understanding everyday life.* Santa Barbara, CA: ABC-CLIO.

Silk, G. (1984). *Automobile and culture.* New York, NY: Harry N. Abrams, Inc.

Smith, M., & Palmer, T. (2008). *Sensing the past: Seeing, hearing, smelling, tasting, and touching in history.* Oakland, CA: University of California Press.

Sofaer, J. R. (2006). *The body as material culture: A theoretical osteoarchaeology.* Cambridge, UK: Cambridge University Press.

Somjee, S. (1993). *Material culture of Kenya.* Nairobi, Kenya: East African Educational Publishers.

Spector, J. (1993). *What this awl means: Feminist archaeology at a Wahpeton Dakota village.* St. Paul, MN: Minnesota Historical Society Press.

Spier, R. F. G. (1973). *Material culture and technology.* Minneapolis, MN: Burgess Publishing Company.

Stark, M. T. (Ed.). (1998). *The archaeology of social boundaries.* Washington, DC: Smithsonian Institution Press.

Stocking, G. W. (1988). *Objects and others: Essays on museums and material culture.* Madison, WI: University of Wisconsin Press.

Stoddard, B. C. (2015). *Steel: From mine to mill, the metal that made America.* Minneapolis, MN: Quarto.

Strasser, S. (1999). *Waste and want: A social history of trash.* New York, NY: Henry Holt and Company.

Thomas, N. (1991). *Entangled objects: Exchange, material culture, and colonialism in the Pacific.* Cambridge, MA: Harvard University Press.
Tilley, C. Y. (Ed.). (1990). *Reading material culture: Structuralism, hermeneutics, and post-structuralism.* Oxford, UK: B. Blackwell.
Tilley, C. Y. (1991). *Material culture and text: The art of ambiguity.* London, UK: Routledge.
Tilley, C. Y. (1999). *Metaphor and material culture.* Oxford, UK: B. Blackwell.
Tilley, C. Y., Keane, W., Kuechler-Fogden, S., Rowlands, M., & Spyer, P. (Eds.). (2006). *Handbook of material culture.* Thousand Oaks, CA: Sage Publications.
Trentmann, F. (2016). *Empire of things: How we became a world of consumers, from the fifteenth century to the twenty-first.* New York, NY: HarperCollins.
Turkle, S. (Ed.). (2007). *Evocative objects: Things we think with.* Cambridge, MA: MIT Press.
Ulrich, L. T. (2001). *The age of homespun: Objects and stories in the creation of an American myth.* New York, NY: Alfred A. Knopf.
Ulrich, L. T., Gaskell, I., Schechner, S. J., & Carter, S. A. (2015). *Tangible things: Making histories through objects.* Oxford, UK: Oxford University Press.
Vannini, P. L. (Ed.). (2009). *Material culture and technology in everyday life.* New York, NY: Peter Lang.
VanStone, J. W. (1992). *Material culture of the Blackfoot (Blood) Indians of southern Alberta.* Chicago, IL: Field Museum of Natural History.
VanStone, J. W. (1993). *Material culture of the Chilcotin Athapaskans of west central British Columbia: Collections in the Field Museum of Natural History.* Chicago, IL: Field Museum of Natural History.
Vare, E. A., & Ptacek, G. (1987). *Mothers of invention: From the bra to the bomb: Forgotten women and their unforgettable ideas.* New York, NY: William Morrow.
Veronese, K. (2015). *Rare: The high stakes race to satisfy our needs for the scarcest metals on Earth.* Amherst, NY: Prometheus.
Walker, R. (2008). *Buying in: What we buy and who we are.* New York, NY: Random House.
Williams, R. (1983). *Culture and society 1780–1950* (2nd ed.). New York, NY: Columbia University.
Williams, R. (2011). *The long revolution.* Westport, CT: Greenwood Press.
Wilson, B. (2013). *Consider the fork: A history of how we cook and eat.* New York, NY: Basic Books.
Witzel, M. K. (1992). *The American gas station: History and folklore of the gas station in American car culture.* New York, NY: Barnes & Noble Books.
Wood, E., & Latham, K. F. (2014). *The objects of experience: Transforming visitor–object encounters in museums.* New York, NY: Routledge.
Woodward, I. (2007). *Understanding material culture.* Los Angeles, CA: Sage Publications.

Wynne-Jones, S. (2016). *A material culture: Consumption and materiality on the coast of precolonial East Africa*. Oxford, UK: Oxford University Press.

References

9/11 Memorial. (n. d.). *The mission*. Available at www.911memorial.org/mission

9/11 Memorial Museum. (2011). Collections management policy. Available at www.911memorial.org/sites/default/files/Collections%20Management%20Policy.pdf

Abrams, J., & Hall, P. (Eds.). (2006). *Else/where: Mapping new cartographies of networks and territories*. Minneapolis, MN: University of Minnesota Design Institute.

Akin, M. (1996). Passionate possession: The formation of private collections. In W. D. Kingery (Ed.), *Learning from things: Method and theory of material culture studies* (pp. 102–128). Washington, DC: Smithsonian.

Anderson, C. W., De Maeyer, J., & Ford, H. (2013, August 5). Ethnographies of objects. *Ethnography matters* [Web log post]. Available at ethnographymatters.net/blog/2013/08/05/august-2013-ethnographies-of-objects/

Anderson, S. W., Damasio, H., & Damasio, A. R. (2005, January). A neural basis for collecting behaviour in humans. *Brain*, 128, 201–212.

Barrett. T. (2003). Interpreting visual culture. *Art Education*, 56(2), 6–12.

Baudrillard, J. (1994). The system of collecting. In J. Elsner & R. Cardinal (Eds.), *The cultures of collecting* (pp. 7–24). Cambridge, MA: Harvard.

Bolin, P. E., & Blandy, D. (2003). Beyond visual culture: Seven statements of support for Material Culture Studies in art education. *Studies in Art Education*, 44(3), 246–263.

Bolin, P. E., & Hoskings, K. (2015). Reflecting on our beliefs and actions: Purposeful practice in art education. *Art Education*, 68(4), 40–47.

Carrington, V. (2012). "There's no going back," Roxie's iPhone: An object ethnography. *Language and Literacy*, 14, 27–40.

Clifford, J. (1988). *The predicament of culture: Twentieth-century ethnography, literature, and art*. Cambridge, MA: Harvard.

Cook, D. (2011, May 7). A blunt critique of game criticism. *Lost garden* [Web blog post]. Available at www.lostgarden.com/search?q=blunt+critique

Csikszentminalyi, M. (1993). Why we need things. In S. Lubar & W. D. Kingery (Eds.), *History from things: Essays on material culture* (pp. 20–29). Washington, DC: Smithsonian.

Danitz, B., & Fein, J. (Directors). (2008). *Objects and memory* [Motion picture]. United States: EVER.

Darts, D. (2004). Visual culture jam: Art, pedagogy, and creative resistance. *Studies in Art Education, 45*(4), 313–327.

Deetz, J. (1977). *In small things forgotten: The archaeology of early American life*. Garden City, NY: Anchor Books.

Dewey, J. (1899). *The school and society*. Chicago, IL: University of Chicago.

Doctorow, C. (2007, July 3). Stasi Smell Museum [Web log post]. Available at boingboing.net/2007/07/03/stasi-smell-museum.html

Duncum, P. (Ed.). (2006). *Visual culture in the art class: Case studies*. Reston, VA: National Art Education Association.

Durbin, G., Morris, S., & Wilkinson, S. (1990). *A teacher's guide to learning from objects*. London, UK: English Heritage.

Evans, J., & Hall, S. (Eds.). (1999). *Visual culture: The reader*. London, UK: Sage.

Farell, S. (Videographer and Producer). (2014). *The keepers of 9/11* [Streaming Video]. Available at www.nytimes.com/video/nyregion/100000002865373/the-keepers-of-911.html

Farver, J. (2006). François Roche and R & Sie(n). In C. Jones (Ed.), *Sensorium: Embodied experience, technology and contemporary art* (pp. 85–90). Cambridge, MA: MIT.

Fleming, E. M. (1974). Artifact study: A proposed model. *Winterthur Portfolio, 9*, 153–173.

Fleming, E. M. (1982). Artifact study: A proposed model. In J. T. Schlereth (Ed.), *Material culture studies in America* (pp. 162–173). Nashville, TN: The American Association for State and Local History.

Ford, H. (2012, January 15). The ethnography of robots. *Ethnography matters* [Web log post]. Available at ethnographymatters.net/blog/2012/01/15/the-ethnography-of-robots/

Forrest, J. (1991). Visual aesthetics for five senses and four dimensions: An ethnographic approach to aesthetic objects. In R. B. Browne & P. Browne (Eds.), *Digging into popular culture: Theories and methodologies in archaeology and other fields* (pp. 48–57). Bowling Green, OH: Bowling Green State University Popular Press.

Freedman, K. (2003). *Teaching visual culture: Curriculum, aesthetics, and the social life of art*. New York, NY: Teachers College Press.

Geahigan, G. (1999). Teaching preservice art education majors: "The world of the work." *Art Education, 52*(5), 12–17.

Gera, N. (2013, July 25). Scents and sensibility: A journey through the world of smell with Sissel Tolaas. *Huffpost Arts & Culture*. Available at www.huffingtonpost.com/nish-gera/sissel-tolaas_b_3647295.html

Gibbs, N. (Ed). (2014). The smarter home. *Time, 184*(1), 2, 48–89.

Gilborn, C. (1968). Pop pedagogy: Looking at the Coke bottle. *Museum News, 47*(4), 12–18.

Glassman, C. (2014, June 2). Making the tough choices: A q & a with curators of the 9/11 museum. *Tribeca Trib Online*. Available at www.tribecatrib.com/content/making-tough-choices-qa-curators-911-museum

Harmon, K. (2003). *You are here*. Princeton, NJ: Princeton Architectural Press.

Hennes, T. (n. d.). Reflections on the opening of the 9/11 Memorial Museum, from the lead exhibition designer [Web log post]. Available at blog.ted.com/2014/05/22/reflections-on-the-opening-of-the-911-memorial-museum-from-the-lead-exhibition-designer/

Huntermann, N. (n. d.). Introduction: Feminist game studies. *Ada: A Journal of Gender and New Media and Technology 2.* doi:10.7264/N37D2S2F. Available at adanewmedia.org/2013/06/issue2-huntemann/

Janson, H. (1991). *History of art* (4th ed.). New York, NY: Harry N. Abrams.

Jones, C. (2006). The mediated sensorium. In C. Jones (Ed.), *Sensorium: Embodied experience, technology and contemporary art* (pp. 5–49). Cambridge, MA: MIT.

Jones, M. O. (1993). Why take a behavioral approach to folk objects? In S. Lubar & W. D. Kingery (Eds.), *History from things: Essays on material culture* (pp. 182–196). Washington, DC: Smithsonian Institution Press.

Keifer-Boyd, K., & Maitland-Gholson, J. (2007). *Engaging visual culture*. Worcester, MA: Davis.

Khanna, P., & Khanna, A. (2011, May 9). Welcome to the Hybrid Age. *Big Think* [Web log post]. Available at bigthink.com/hybrid-reality/welcome-to-the-hybrid-age

Kimmelman, M. (2014, May 28). Finding space for the living at a memorial. *The New York Times*. Available at www.nytimes.com/2014/05/29/arts/design/finding-space-for-the-living-at-a-memorial.html

Kingery, W. D. (1993). Technological systems with some implications with regard to continuity and change. In S. Lubar & W. D. Kingery (Eds.), *History from things: Essays on material culture* (pp. 215–230). Washington, DC: Smithsonian.

Kingery, W. D. (Ed.). (1996). *Learning from things: Method and theory of material culture studies*. Washington, DC: Smithsonian Institution Press.

KirbyKid. (2008, July 7). How to write a critical game review. *Critical gaming* [Web log post]. Available at critical-gaming.blogspot.com/2008/07/how-to-write-critical-video-game-review.html

Knappett, C. (2005). *Thinking through material culture: An interdisciplinary perspective*. Philadelphia, PA: University of Pennsylvania Press.

Kopytoff, I. (1986). The biography of things. In A. Appadurai (Ed.), *The social life of things: Commodities in cultural perspective* (pp. 64–91). Cambridge, UK: Cambridge University Press.

Lassiter, L. E. (2004). Collaborative ethnography. *Anthronotes, 25*, 1–9.

Lavin, I. (1983). The art of art history. *ARTnews, 82*(8), 96–101.

Lubar, S. (1996). Learning from technological things. In W. David Kingery (Ed.), *Learning from things: Method and theory of material culture studies* (pp. 31–34). Washington, DC: Smithsonian Institution Press.

Martin, A. S., & Garrison, J. R. (Eds.). (1997). *American material culture: The shape of the field*. Winterthur, DE: The Henry Francis du Pont Winterthur Museum.

McFee, J. K. (1970). *Preparation for art* (2nd ed.). Belmont, CA: Wadsworth.

McGrane, S. (2007, April 24). The odor artist. *Wired Magazine*. Available at archive.wired.com/wired/archive/15.05/posts_odor.html

McLuhan, M., & McLuhan, E. (1988). *Laws of media*. Toronto, Canada: University of Toronto.

Mirzoeff, N. (2009). *An introduction to visual culture*. New York, NY: Routledge.

Mirzoeff, N. (2012). *The visual culture reader* (3rd ed.). London, UK: Routledge.

Mitchell, W. J. T. (2005). *What do pictures want? The lives and loves of images*. Chicago, IL: University Press of Chicago.

Montgomery, C. F. (1982). The connoisseurship of artifacts. In T. J. Schlereth (Ed.), *Material culture studies in America* (pp. 143–152). Nashville, TN: The American Association for State and Local History.

Nemeth, J. (2011). The practice of collecting: Private worlds of youth culture and a rationale for art curriculum. In P. E. Bolin & D. Blandy (Eds.), *Matter matters: Art education and material culture studies* (pp. 126–132). Reston, VA: National Art Education Association.

Olson, A., & Olson, B. (2014, July 19). WPA ceramics. *North Dakota Pottery Collectors Society*. Available at www.ndpcs.org/wpa.htm

Prown, J. D., & Haltman, K. (Eds.). (2000). *American artifacts: Essays in material culture*. East Lansing, MI: Michigan State University Press.

Root-Bernstein, M., & Root-Bernstein, R. (2011, July 31). Childhood collecting: A neglected connection between playing and learning. *Psychology Today*. Available at www.psychologytoday.com/blog/imagine/201107/childhood-collecting-neglected-connection-between-playing-and-learning

Rose, D. (2014). *Enchanted objects: Design, human desire, and the Internet of things*. New York, NY: Scribner.

Sarkeesian, A. (n. d.). *Feminist frequency* [Web post]. Available at www.feministfrequency.com/

Schlereth, T. J. (1992). *Cultural history and material culture: Everyday life, landscapes, museums*. Charlottesville, VA: University Press of Virginia.

Schlereth, T. J. (Ed.). (1985). *Material culture: A research guide*. Lawrence, KS: University Press of Kansas.

Sheumaker, H., & Wajda, S. T. (Eds.). (2008). *Material culture in America: Understanding everyday life*. Santa Barbara, CA: ABC-CLIO.

Star, S. L. (1999). The ethnography of infrastructure. *American Behavioral Scientist, 43*, 377–391.

Sterling, B. (2012, February). An architect's wet-cement dream: Just as termites build castles on earth, robots could erect skyscrapers on the moon. *Wired*. Available at www.wired.com/2005/02/an-architects-wet-cement-dream/

Stott, M. A. (1987). Object, context and process: Approaches to teaching about material culture. In B. Reynolds & M. A. Stott (Eds.), *Material anthropology: Contemporary approaches to material culture* (pp. 13–30). Lanham, MD: University Press of America.

References

Sturken, M., & Cartwright, L. (2001). *Practices of looking: An introduction to visual culture*. London, UK: Routledge.

Tavin, K. M. (2003). Wrestling with angels, searching for ghosts: Toward a critical pedagogy of visual culture. *Studies in Art Education, 44*(3), 197–213.

Taylor, P. (2007). Press pause: Critically contextualizing music video in visual culture and art education. *Studies in Art Education, 48*(3), 230–246.

Tilley, C., Keane, W., Kuechler, S., Rowlands, M., & Spyer, P. (Eds.). (2006). *Handbook of material culture*. London, UK: Sage.

Turkle, S. (Ed.). (2007). *Evocative objects: Things we think with*. Cambridge, MA: MIT Press.

Vannini, P. L. (2009). Material culture studies and the sociology and anthropology of technology. In P. L. Vannini (Ed.), *Material culture and technology in everyday life: Ethnographic approaches* (pp. 15–26). New York, NY: Peter Lang.

Vogel, C. (2008, April 11). 2 plucky collectors, 50 lucky museums. *The New York Times*. Available at www.nytimes.com/2008/04/11/arts/design/11voge.html

Waddington, D. I. (2010). Scientific self-defense: Transforming Dewey's idea of technological transparency. *Educational Theory, 60*(5), 621–638.

Warhol, A. (1975). *The philosophy of Andy Warhol*. New York, NY: Harcourt Brace

Woodward, I. (2009). Material culture and narrative: Fusing myth, materiality, and meaning. In P. L. Vannini (Ed.), *Material culture and technology in everyday life: Ethnographic approaches* (pp. 59–72). New York, NY: Peter Lang.

Zlatanovski, D. (n.d.). About the typology. Typology. Available at www.thetypology.com/ABOUT-THE-TYPOLOGY

Index

Abrams, J., 99
Access points, in object study, 96–97
ACCIDENTAL MYSTERIES (website), 45
Activities. See Learning activities
Adaptive relationship, art–technology, 72
Akin, M., 43
Alienated relationship, art–technology, 72
Anderson, C. W., 68
Anderson, S. W., 40
Anthropology, biography within, 69–70
Appraisal, of objects, 10, 28, 97
Approaches, in material culture study
   biography within anthropology, 69–70
   information acquisition and learning and, 24–25
   metaphoric, 23–24
   specific to different fields, 93–101
   story/storytelling, 33–37
   teaching and, 87–101 (See also Instructional strategies; Learning activities)
   to technology, 66–67
   variation in, 25
   via fieldwork, 89–91
   to videogames and virtual environments, 73–74
Approaches, to objects. See also Object study
   five-step investigation, 100–101
   life-story association, exploring, 34–37
   multisensory, 98
   object as storyteller, 33–34
   personal significance, investigating, 29–30
   question-driven research, 30–31
   repurposing, 32–33
   search value and, 31–32
Art
   change in character of, 77–78
   multisensory (See Multisensory art)
   public vs. private collections, 42
   visual (See Visual art)
Art education
   children's collecting behavior and, 41
   material culture and, books relating to, 103–113
   material culture confluence with, 13–15
   multisensory art and, 85–86
   multisensory elements in, 20–21
Artifacts. See Object(s)
   hands-on learning examples (See Object investigation (case examples))
   study of (See Object study)

Artists
  as cultural seers, 71
  and emergence of multisensory art, 77–78
  multisensory, 78–84 (*See also individually named artists*)
Artphones. *See* Smartphones/artphones

Baker, Bridget, *So it Goes* (installation), 79
Barrett. T., 76
Battements et Papillons (installation), 81–82
Baudrillard, J., 40
Bearing witness, collecting/collections as, 45–48
Bibliography, material culture and art eduction, 103–113
BioArt, 21
Biography. *See* Life stories
Blandy, D., 3, 20
  early exposure to collecting/collections, 1
  fieldwork approach to material culture study, 89–91
Blind Light (installation), 83
Blog(s)
  of Anita Sarkeesian, 74
  TYPOLOGIST, 44
Bolin, Madeleine (author's daughter), 55
Bolin, P. E., 3, 13, 20
  early exposure to collecting/collections, 1
Buehler, Markus J., work of, 21
"Butterscotch dog" (ceramic object), 38–39

Cabinets of curiosities, 42–43
Calder, Alexander (artist), 75–76
Carrington, V., 68
Cartwright, L., 22
Catastrophic events, institutional collecting response to, 45–48
Chinese folktales (object investigation example), 50, 58–62
Classification, in material culture study, 94–95
Clifford, J., 40, 41
Coin collection, 39
Collaborative ethnography, in object study, 98–99
Collectibles, on Essy, 43
Collecting/Collections
  authors' early exposure to, 1
  authors' own, 38–40
  bearing witness to catastrophic events, 45–48
  and hoarding distinguished, 41
  impulse for, 40–41
  management policy at 9/11 Memorial Museum, 47
  passion for, 40–42
  public *vs*. private, 42
  significance of, 19–20, 38–40
  smells, 43
  of students (activity), 98
  typology of, 43–45
  ubiquitous nature of, 40–42
Collective memory, role in material culture studies, 19
Constructed environments, value of studying, 24–25
Construction, object study and, 96
Consumer, handcrafted objects and, 95
Context, in material culture study, 93–94
Cook, D., 73
Csikszentminalyi, M., 40
Cultural analysis, in object study, 96

Curators
  multisensory, 84
  at National 9/11 Memorial Museum, 46
  at Royal Academy of Arts, London, 73–84 (*See also individually named curators*)
Customization, personal (activity), 93

Damasio, A. R., 40
Damasio, H., 40
Danitz, B., 46, 47
Darts, D., 76
Daughters of Edward Darla Boot (painting), 51–53
Davis Brody Bon and Snohetta (architects), 45–46
De Maeyer, J., 68
Dead-end reflecting activity, 31–32
Deduction, in object exploration, 100
Deetz, J., 28–29, 37
Description/Descriptive operation
  in material culture study, 94–95
  in object exploration, 100
Design
  multisensory influences in, 21
  of object, evolutionary changes in (activity), 89
  as property in object study, 96
Design Observer Group (web page), 45
Dewey, J., 65–66, 70
Dion, Mark (artist), 42–43
Discarding objects, 27
Displaying objects, 27
Doctorow, C., 43
"Dolls and Dummies" (video installation), 81
Domestication, of technology, 64–65
Dream car contest, 44
Drones, 64
Duncum, P., 76
Durbin, G., 101

Ethnography
  collaborative, in object study, 98–99
  object, 68–69
  personal (activity), 92–93
Ethnography Matters (website), 68–69
Etsy, collectibles on, 43
Evaluation, of objects
  comparative, 96
  monetary value, 10, 28, 97
Evans, J., 22
Evolutionary changes, in object design (activity), 89
Exercises. *See* Learning activities
Existence. *See* Human existence/Humanity
Experiences, sensory contact and, 49

Farrell, S., 46
Farver, J., 72
Fein, J., 46, 47
Feminist perspective, videogames and, 74
Fenn, J., fieldwork approach to material culture study, 89–91
Fieldwork, orientation to (activity), 89–91
Fleming, E. M., 32, 95–96
Flight 93, selecting artifacts from, 48
Folktales, Chinese (object investigation example), 50
Ford, H., 68
Forrest, J., 98
Foster, J. (Internet collector), 45

Freedman, K., 22, 76
Fresh Kills Landfill, Staten Island, NY, 47
Function of object
　intended and unintended, 32–33
　as property in object study, 96
Future, material culture in the, imagining (activity), 91–92

Game(s)
　instructional, 88–89
　videogames, 73–74
Garrison, J. R., 16
Gauthier, Jean-Pierre, *Battements et Papillons* (installation), 81–82
Geahigan, G., 33
Geiger, S. (researcher), 68
Gender politics, videogames and, 74
Gera, N., 43
Gibbs, N., 63
Gilborn, C., 94–95
Glassman, C., 47, 48
González-Torres, Felix, *"Untitled" (Portrait of Ross in L.A.)* (installation), 82
Goodwin, Kate, "Sensing Spaces: Architecture Reimagined" (installation), 83–84
Google Glass, 64
Gormley, Antony, *Blind Light* (installation), 83
Grief, institutional collecting in midst of, 45–48

Hall, P., 99
Hall, S., 22
Haltman, K., 100
Handcrafted objects, investigating, 95
Harmon, K., 99
Hearing
　memory triggered by, 28
　in object-reflective narrative, 33–34
Hennes, T., 46
Herbert and Dorothy Vogel private collection, 42
Hidden objects, 27
History, in object study, 96
Hoarding, and collecting distinguished, 41
Höller, Carsten, *Test Site* (installation), 80
Hoskings, K., 13
Human existence/Humanity, 65
　Hybrid Age of, 63–64
　objects as essence of, 28–29
　technology intersection with, 64–66
Human senses. *See* Senses
Huntermann, N., 74
Hybrid Age
　artists' responses to, 71–73
　characteristics of, 63
　technology and material culture examples in, 63–64

iPod, 67
Ideas, for object analysis, 101
Identification, in object study, 96
Imaginative self-reflection (exercise), 33
Immerse relationship, art–technology, 72
Individual memory, role in Material culture studies, 19
Installations, multisensory, 78–84. *See also individually named artists and/or installations*
　phobic responses to, 72, 83
Institutional collecting, 45–48
Institutional collecting/collections
　art, 42

in response to catastrophic events, 45–48
Instructional strategies, 87–93. *See also* Learning activities
Intended functions, of objects, 32–33
Interdisciplinary nature, of material culture studies, 16–17
Internet, collectors and collecting on, 43–45
"Internet of Things," 71
Interpretive analysis/operation
  in approach to material culture study, 94
  in object study/exploration, 96, 100–101
Interrogative relationship, art–technology, 72

Jackson, K. (president, New-York Historical Society), 46
Jason, H., 79
Johnston, Waldo and Hazel (author's grandparents), 1
Jones, C., 71, 72–73
Jones, M. O., 95

Keane, W., 8
Keefe, Kathryn (author's relative), 57
Keefer-Boyd, K., 76
Khanna, A., 63
Khanna, P., 63
Kienholz, Edward, *The State Hospital* (installation), 78–79
Kimmelman, M., 46
Kingery, W. D., 14, 65, 66
KirbyKid, on writing videogame reviews, 73–74
Knappett, C., 17
Knowledge, collections as source of, 41
Kopytoff, I., 69–70
Kuechler, S., 8

Lanier, Vincent (art educator), 2
Lassiter, L. E., 68–69, 73, 98–99
Latour, Bruno, 65–66
Lavin, I., 14
Learning activities, 34
  dead-end searches, 31–32
  evolutionary changes in object design, 89
  fieldwork orientation, 89–91
  identifying objects, structures, and spaces, 89
  imaginative self-reflection, 33–34
  imagining future material culture, 91–92
  life-story association with object, 34–37
  object analysis, framework of ideas and questions for, 101
  objects and spaces in literature, 88
  personal customization, 93
  personal ethnography, 92–93
  personal significance of object, investigating, 29–30
  question-driven research, 30–31
  SCRAP This Assignment (game), 88–89
  student collecting/collections, 88
  use *vs.* role of object, 32–33
  "Who Made That?" strategy, 92
Life stories
  in material culture exploration, recognizing value of, 17–18
  and object association, 27–37 (*See also* Learning activities)
  of things, 69–70
Location, investigations involving, 49–62
  rocking chair example, 50, 53–58

Location, investigations involving (*continued*)
  traditional Chinese folktales example, 50, 58–62
Lubar, S., 65, 66

Maitland-Gholson, J., 76
Making things, 22
Mapping, of multisensory environments, 99–100
Martin, A. S., 16
Material, in object study, 96
Material culture
  art education and, books relating to, 103–113
  collecting/collections and (*See* Collecting/Collections)
  concepts encompassing, 8–12
  confluence with art education, 13–15
  defined, 3
  exclusions, 12–13
  future, imagining (activity), 91–92
  human senses and, perceiving connection between, 20–21
  investigating, five-step approach to, 100–101
  and material culture studies distinguished, 16
  multisensory characteristics of, 43
  objects and spaces in, making and responding to, 22
  political nature of, understanding and appreciating, 18–19
  story in exploration of, value in, 17–18
  study of (*See* Material culture study)
  subjectivity and, 40
  technology and, 63–74 (*See also* Technology)
  use of term, 16

Material culture study
  development of, 2–3
  evolving pedagogy in, 2
  fieldwork approach to, 89–91
  interdisciplinary nature of, 16–17
  key ideas in, 2–3, 15–25
  material culture distinguished from, 16
  metaphoric approaches in, discerning, 23–24
  role of memory in, 19
  teaching approaches and strategies, 87–101 (*See also* Instructional strategies; Learning activities)
  technology integral to, 65–66
  use of term, 16
  value of, support for, 24–25
  variable approaches to, exploring, 25
  visual culture and, differences and similarities between, 21
Material Culture Typology (Internet publication), 45
McFee, J. K., 2, 14
McGrane, S., 43
McLuhan, E., 70
McLuhan, M., 70
Media effects, tetrad of, 70
Memory
  individual and collective, role of, 19–20
  photographs triggering, in rocking chair investigation, 57
  senses triggering, 28
Metaphoric approaches, in material culture studies, 23–24
Mirzoeff, N., 22
Mitchell, W. J. T., 17
Montgomery, C. F., 96–97
Morris, S., 101
Mott, Iain, and Marc Raszewski,

Summoned Voices (installation), 79–80
Multisensory art
  art education and, 85–86
  artists/curators, 78–84 (*See also* individually named artists and curators)
  events/exhibitions, 84–85
  technology and, taxonomy for, 72–73
  virtual/physical sites about, 84
Multisensory elements/influences
  in approach to object study, 98
  in art and design, 20–21, 43
  of material culture, 43, 49
Multisensory environments, mapping of, 99–100
Multisensory installations, 78–84. *See also* individually named artists and/or installations
Museum collections
  art, 42
  9/11 artifacts, 45–48

Narrative(s)
  object-reflective, senses involved in, 33–34
  in rocking chair investigation, 58
  technology and, 67–68
National 9/11 Memorial Museum, 45–48
  collections management policy, 47
Neanderthals, research on, 25
Nemeth, J., 41
Neperud, Ron (art educator), 2
Neto, Ernesto, walkthrough installations of, 80–81
New York City Municipal Archive, 46
New-York Historical Society, 46
9/11 Memorial, 45
9/11 Memorial Museum, 47. *See also* National 9/11 Memorial Museum
1984 (Orwell), 88

Object(s)
  abundance of, 27
  approaches to, 29–37 (*See also* Approaches, to objects)
  discarding, 27
  displaying *vs.* hiding, 27
  as essence of existence, 28–29
  evolutionary changes in (activity), 89
  function of (*See* Function of object)
  gathering of (*See* Collecting/Collections)
  hands-on learning about (*See* Object investigation (case examples))
  important, identifying (activity), 89
  investigating personal significance of, 29–30
  life stories associated with, 27–37
  in literature (activity), 98
  making and responding to, 22
  properties of, 96
  repurposing, 32–33
  as storyteller, 33–34
  studying (*See* Object study)
  technological, 66
  as visual art, 75
  worth of, 27–28
Object ethnography, 68–69
Object investigation (case examples)
  animated book of traditional Chinese folktales, 50, 58–62
  rocking chair, 50, 53–58
Object-reflective narrative, senses in, 33–34

Object study
  access points in, 96–97
  as approach to material culture study, 93–94
  benefits of, 49–50
  five-step approach to, 100–101
  framework for analysis in, 101
  hands-on, examples of (*See* Object investigation (case examples))
  operational phases in, 96
  spanning time, people, and location, 49–62
  tangible objects, value of, 24–25
Olson, A., 39
Olson, B., 39
Orientation to fieldwork (activity), 89–91
Orwell, George, *1984*, 88
Oursler, Tony, "Dolls and Dummies" (video installation), 81

Passion, for collecting, 40–42
Pedagogy
  material culture studies, 2
  relationship between collecting and, 41
People, investigations involving, 49–62
  traditional Chinese folktales example, 50, 58–62
Personal customization (activity), 93
Personal ethnography (activity), 92–93
Personal significance, of object (activity), 29–30
Photographs, use in rocking chair investigation, 55–58
Physical objects
  as connectors, 58
  value of studying, 24–25
Pinterest, 45
Points of access, in object study, 96–97
Political nature, of material culture, 18–19
Private collecting/collections
  art, 42
  in response to catastrophic events, 45–48
Process, in material culture study, 93–94
Producer, of handcrafted objects, 95
Product–producer interface, handcrafted objects and, 95
Prown, J. D., 100
Public collecting/collections
  art, 42
  in response to catastrophic events, 45–48

Question-driven research (activity), 30–31
Questions
  for critique of videogames and virtual environments, 73–74
  for object analysis, 101
  for study of technology, 70–71
Quilts, multisensory approach to, 98

Ramirez, J. (curator), 46, 47, 48
Raszewski, Marc, and Iain Mott, *Summoned Voices* (installation), 79–80
Read, Hugh and Jenevieve (author's grandparents), 54
Read, Max (author's relative), 57
Read, Ruth (author's aunt), 56
Recontextualization of objects, collecting/collections and, 40, 42–43

Repurposing objects, 32–33
Research, in object exploration, 100
Residual relationship, art–technology, 72
Resistant relationship, art–technology, 72
Resources, selected books on material culture and art eduction, 103–113
Responding to objects, 22
Robotic devices, 64
Roche, Francois (conceptual architect), 71, 72
Rocking chair (object investigation example), 50, 53–58
Role of object, use *vs.* (activity), 32–33
Root-Bernstein, M., 41
Root-Bernstein, R., 41
Rose, D., 71
Rowlands, M., 8
R&Sie(n), 71

Sargent, John Singer, *Daughters of Edward Darley Boit*, 51–53
Sarkeesian, A., 74
Schlereth, T. J., 2, 7, 12, 16
SCRAP This Assignment (game), 88–89
Self, artifacts and, 40
Self-reflection, imaginative (exercise), 33
Senses. *See also individually named senses; Multisensory entries*
  connections between material culture and, 20–21
  experiences and, 49
  memory triggered by, 28
  in object-reflective narrative, 33–34
"Sensing Spaces: Architecture Reimagined" (installation), 83–84
Sensorium: Embodied Experience, Technology, and Contemporary Art (Jones), 71
Sheumaker, H., 8, 9
Sight
  memory triggered by, 28
  in object-reflective narrative, 33–34
"The Smarter Home: . . ." (*Time* report), 63
Smartphones/artphones, 63–64
  biography of, 69–70
  McLuhan's tetrad applied to, 70–71
  narratives associated with, 67–68
  systems approach to study of, 66–67
Smell(s)
  collections of, 43
  memory triggered by, 28
  in object-reflective narrative, 33–34
Smell and the City (website), 43
So it Goes (installation), 79
Spaces
  analytic approaches to, 25
  constructed environments as, value of studying, 24–25
  human-made, identifying (activity), 89
  in literature (activity), 88
  making and responding to, 22
  metaphoric approaches to, discerning, 23–24
Speculation, in object exploration, 100
Spyer, P., 8
Star, S. L., 68
The State Hospital (installation), 78–79

Sterling, B., 71–72
Stories, related to objects. *See also* Life stories
  exploration approach to, 34–37
  object as storyteller approach, 33–34
Storyteller, object as, 33–34
Stott, M. A., 93–94
Structures, human-made, identifying (activity), 89
Sturken, M., 22
Subjectivity, material culture and, 40
Summoned Voices (installation), 79–80
Systems approach, to technology, 66–67

Tangible objects, value of studying, 24–25
Taste
  memory triggered by, 28
  in object-reflective narrative, 33–34
Tavin, K. M., 76
Taxonomy, for art–technology relationship, 72–73
Taylor, Laura Hughes (ceramicist), 38–39
Taylor, P., 76
A Teacher's Guide: Exploring Material Culture in the Classroom (PBS), 69
A Teacher's Guide to Learning from Objects (Durbin, Morris & Wilkinson), 101
Teaching
  instructional strategies for, 87–93
  learning activities and (*See* Learning activities)
Technology
  biography of things and, 69–70
  coexisting trajectories, 71
  defined, 63
  emotional response to, 71
  handcrafted objects and, 95
  human intersection with, 64–66
  Hybrid Age and, 71–72
  making sense of, taxonomy for, 72–73
  material culture examples, 63–64
  McLuhan's tetrad applied to, 70–71
  narrative and, 67–68
  new, adapting to, 64–65
  object ethnography and, 68–69
  systems approach to, 66–67
Test Site (installation), 80
Tetrad of media effects, 70
Things. *See also* Object(s)
  biography of, 69–70
  making, 22
Tilley, C., 8
Time, investigations spanning, 49–62
  rocking chair example, 50, 53–58
Tolaas, Sissel (odor artist), 43
Touch
  memory triggered by, 28
  in object-reflective narrative, 33–34
Traditional Chinese folktales (object investigation example), 58–62
Tropes vs. Women in Video Games (video), 74
Turkle, S., 30
TYPOLOGIST (blog), 44
Typology, defined, 44
TYPOLOGY (website/social media), 43–44

Understanding, collections as source of, 41

Unintended functions, of objects, 32–33
"Untitled" (Portrait of Ross in L.A.) (installation), 82
urunderkammers, 42–43
Use of object, role *vs.* (activity), 32–33

Vannini, P. L., 64
Videogames, 73–74
Virtual environments, 73–74
Visual art/Visual culture
   material culture studies and, differences and similarities between, 21, 42–43
   regard for, 75–77
   transition to multisensory engagement, 77–78
Vogel, C., 42
Vogel, Herbert and Dorothy (private art collectors), 42

Waddington, D. I., 65
Wajda, S. T., 8, 9
Warhol, A., 43
"Who Made That?" (activity), 92
Wilkinson, S., 101
The Wolf and the Dough Children (object investigation example), 50, 58–62
Women, representation in videogames, 74
Woodward, I., 9, 67
Works Project Administration (WPA), 38–39
World Trade Center, New York City
   9/11 Memorial Museum on site of, 45–48
   attacks on, 45

Zlatanovski, D., 43–44
   typology displays by, 44–45

About the Authors

Doug Blandy is a professor in the College of Design at the University of Oregon.

Paul E. Bolin is a professor in the Department of Art and Art History at The University of Texas at Austin.